I *already* AM

TESTIMONIES OF BELIEF IN THE GREAT I AM

Michelle J. Goff

Iron Rose Sister Ministries
Searcy, Arkansas

Michelle J. Goff / CreateSpace
Iron Rose Sister Ministries
www.IronRoseSister.com
1-501-593-4849

Book Layout ©2013 BookDesignTemplates.com

I *already* AM / Michelle J. Goff.—1st ed.
ISBN 978-1-7340293-0-7

Contents

i

Dedicated to Team Goff
(A.K.A., my parents)

Through our imperfections, trials, strengths, and weaknesses, along every step of the journey, we respect, support, and love each other, no matter what.

You are truly "partners in the gospel" (Phil. 1:5). And God's answers to your prayers for others to serve in that way are what have made this book possible.

Thank you for always teaching me—through your words and your examples—to seek and give glory to the I AM. I thank Him for putting us on the same team, with Him as the Captain. And I thank you for your countless revisions and feedback along every tedious step of the way with this book— and oh, so much more!

Geaux Team!

Acknowledgements

Katie Forbess, the glorified cheerleader, exemplary Iron Rose Sister, fearless Team Leader and forever friend. I thank God for the mutual blessing of our friendship and teamwork in the kingdom.

Thank you to the women who attended the pilot study of this book at the Downtown Church of Christ. I looked forward to every Wednesday night, valued your feedback, and cherished our time together with the I AM.

Brenda, Erica, Debora, Wendy, Amanda, and others on the Iron Rose Sister Ministries Team, without the roles that each of you played, I would not have had the time, energy, or mental bandwidth to allow the I AM to speak through me on the pages of this book. Speaking for myself, and on behalf of the women who will deepen their belief in the I AM and relationships with other Iron Rose Sisters, thank you!

Thank you to the Iron Rose Sister Ministries Board of Directors for encouraging and enforcing a more balanced work-life balance so that I could continue to allow God to use my passions for writing, teaching, and speaking to His glory. It is a blessing to be able to "stay in my lane."

Special thanks are also extended to Jordan Yarbrough and the Goad family for helping me get away for a few days to write, edit, revise, and recharge.

This book is dedicated to my parents, who have always provided unconditional support. Yet the shout-out of thanks to my family would be incomplete without my sisters and brothers-in-law. Thank you for your constant prayers, support, and patience, especially when I am in "writing mode." You each inspire a better version of who the I AM is in me. And I love doing family life with you!

Also, thank you to Kadesh and Zeni for the ever-inspiring stories and insights into the I AM that you provide through a child's eyes of belief.

Finally, to the I AM, who was, is and always will be the constant in my life. Thank you for being. And thank you for making possible all of the being and doing that I have acknowledged above, and so much more. To You be the honor and the glory throughout all generations, forever and ever. Amen.

P.S. To my other editors: George Brown (A.K.A. Granddaddy), Christa Duve, and Carla Sumner... Did you think I forgot you? No way! This book cannot become what it is as an instrument in the Great I AM's hands without your meticulous revision. Thank you for being a part of the team that equips women to connect to the I AM and to one another more deeply through this book.

Additional thanks to Kendra Neill for book cover brainstorming, Ken Mills for the cover design, and Geoffrey Wyatt for the profile picture.

Iron Rose Sister Ministries Bible Studies Format

The Iron Rose Sister Ministries (IRSM) Bible Studies are designed for a small group context. Even if it were possible for me to give you "all the answers" and share my perspective on the verses and concepts being presented, it cannot be emphasized enough the value of fellowship, discussion, and prayer with other Christian sisters! The format of the IRSM Bible Studies allows for greater discussion, depth of insight, and sharing of unique perspectives. If you don't follow the book exactly, that's ok! You are invited to make the studies your own, to allow the Spirit to lead, and to treat the studies as a guide and a resource, not a script.

The IRSM Bible Studies also provide the opportunity for spiritual journaling on a personal level by making note of the date you complete each chapter and by adding notes in the margins, in addition to answering the questions.

The 'Common Threads' (pictured on the next page) will also allow you to chronicle your personal growth individually and in communion with your Iron Rose Sisters. Using the image of the rose and the IRSM logo, the bloom of the rose represents areas we come to recognize in which we long to grow. Through these studies, we can also identify thorns we'd like to work on removing or need help to remove. They may be thorns like Paul's (2 Cor. 12:7-10), but by identifying them; we can know where they are and either dull them or stop sticking others and ourselves with them. The final Common Thread is the iron, which is best defined and facilitated in communion with other Christian sisters, Iron Rose Sisters.

Common Threads in IRSM Studies

how you'd like
to grow and bloom

a thorn you'd
like to remove

an area in which you are striving
to dig deeper or need to have
someone hold you accountable

What is an Iron Rose Sister?

An Iron Rose Sister is a Christian sister who serves as iron sharpening iron (Prov. 27:17), encouraging and inspiring others to be as beautiful as a rose in spite of a few thorns.

Purposes of Iron Rose Sister Relationships:

➤ Encouragement and inspiration
➤ Prayer
➤ Understanding and affirmation
➤ Confidentiality
➤ Spiritual audit (IRS = Iron Rose Sister)
➤ Mutual call to holy living
➤ Spiritual friendship and conversation

Recommendations for Iron Rose Sister Ministries Bible Studies:

➤ Allow for an hour to an hour and a half meeting time weekly.
  o We're women—we like to talk!
  o Prayer time
  o Depth of conversation and discussion
➤ Rotate facilitating the weekly discussion among EACH of the women.
  o Everyone can lead!
  o Everyone will grow!
  o Additional suggestions and recommendations are found in the *Facilitator's Guide (pg. 203)*
➤ Commit to reading the chapter ahead of time.
  o The discussion will be richer and deeper if everyone comes prepared.
  o How much you put in will be directly proportional to how much you get out.
  o You will need to do these studies with your favorite Bible in hand.
  o All verses, unless otherwise noted, are quoted from the English Standard Version (ESV).
➤ Follow up with each other during the week.
  o Prayer
  o Encouragement
  o 'Common Threads'

The IRSM logo designation is used to highlight questions that lend themselves to good group discussion: ice-breakers, questions for depth of insight or additional perspectives, and areas for growth and sharing.

I *already* AM
Testimonies of Belief in the Great I AM

Introduction

Every woman has her creative process. Yes, everyone! My mom would argue that she is not "creative" enough to have a process, but the way she creates a lesson plan for special needs children, or creates a meal, tips the argument in my favor.

My creative process for writing always begins with a struggle. God and I wrestle over something and the truth He reveals becomes the focus for the next book. My motivation is to prevent others from going through the pain of my struggles and to teach the lessons I had to beat my head against a wall to learn.

Through the wrestling, like Jacob, I leave with a limp, which then becomes my testimony of belief in God—who He is and what He is actively doing in my life. I then hope to lead with the limp and point others to the Healer, Comforter, Redeemer, Guide, Friend, and the many other names and eternal qualities of the I AM we will explore through this book.

But back to the creative process... As a result of the struggle, the heart of the lesson learned usually centers around a title. In this case, I already AM was as clear to me as any title has ever been. In Chapter 1, I tell the story of how the title came about, but don't skip ahead yet. Hang with me on the journey to introduce the direction God has taken this book.

My constant prayer is that God will guide my thoughts, my words, my prayers, my study, and every aspect of what gets put on the page.

> *An authentic, transparent narrative of my own journey becomes an invitation to others in their journeys.*

And just as David continued to consult with God along his journey, in contrast to Saul who ran with the first instruction he thought he understood (1 Sam. 23; 1 Chron. 10:14), it is important to seek God's guidance continually, especially in our creative processes.

For me, the subtitle is one of the next initial steps in the creative process—not that a subtitle is necessary. However, for me, it is the sub-theme that cohesively weaves throughout each chapter and brings us back to the main point. It usually rises to the surface in the process of seeking God's guidance, gathering my notes, collecting my thoughts, and developing an outline for the book's contents.

However, for this book, the process of landing on a subtitle became an illustration of my struggle with God on the very topic this book addresses—keeping the I AM at the center of it all. Wrestling with myself, verbally processing with others, and crying out to God to make it clear, were all part of the arduous process.

Wordsmithing is fun for me, but I was lost in the tension of trying to fit a square peg into a round hole. No word would work; no phrasing would function; no statement was sufficiently stunning. Trusting that God would bring a breakthrough and revelation of truth, I leaned into and welcomed the tension instead of avoiding it.

The Crazy Train of Thought Back to the I AM

Travel with me on the train of thought where God led me in order to bring me back to what it truly was all about (and what became our approach to this study of the I AM):

I started with the I AM statements in John... If Christ Himself proclaimed who He was in these ways, it must be important to focus on those attributes of His eternal nature. And we can see from the reaction of others **the significance of His I AM declarations was equality with the God of the Old Testament** (John 8:58). Wow!

Then, turning back to Exodus 3 brought a reexamination of the first time that God declares Himself to be the I AM. Oooooh, through Moses' conversation with God, he is given purpose, identity, and redemption. Yes! We all want some of that! Maybe that is the hook for this book: finding purpose and identity, or answers to whatever questions we are seeking—through belief in the I AM. Awesome!

Closer to a breakthrough of understanding, I returned to my nauseatingly long list of variations on the subtitle, which still reflected a disconnect:

> ➢ "Lessons in Fulfillment from the Great I AM" Nope. Wrong focus.

> ➢ "Knowing and Believing in His Name" Closer...

> ➢ "Confident Belief in the Limitless I AM" Maybe...

> ➢ "Believing I AM's Perspective on Life" But it's more than that!

> ➢ "Affirmation and Clarification from the Great I AM" Drifting and reaching again...

> ➢ "How the Great I AM defines purpose, identity, and perspective" Ugh, back to a selfish focus.

While catchy and holding various levels of potential, these and all of the other possible subtitles were inadequate, imperfect, incomplete, and lacking... words which mirrored my feelings about myself.

Dejected, I flipped back through the folder of my early notes, praying that God would return the zeal for this book and make things clear. Stumbling on the hand-written page with the definitive title "I *already* AM," and a verse written in large letters, I opened my Bible to re-read the verse written at the bottom of that page: John 8:58. *"Jesus said to them, 'Truly, truly, I say to you, before Abraham was, I AM.'"*

Simple as that. Truthfully stated by the One who embodies truth; a statement of existence from the One who created life: I AM.

That was when it hit me: It was the same trap God had directed me to address through this book. The true focus was lost in a selfish search for identity, purpose, provision, fulfillment, and answers... things we think we need and fruitlessly seek throughout our lives. A desire to answer the questions women across the Americas are asking drove me, but it led me into a prideful aspiration to write the best-selling book that would equip countless women to connect to the I AM.

My focus was flawed. My desire to answer life's questions and inspire you to believe in the I AM through a subtitle was confused.

How easy it was to lose sight of the I AM. His very existence, His being, the One who was and is and is to come, had to be the center of it all. In the same way that the I AM incarnate stirred the crowd with His response in John 8:58, it stirred and convicted me at the realization of how far one can wander from the I AM, even in an effort to point others to Him.

> *The I AM, the One Who Reveals,*
> *patiently began to reveal Himself to me again—just as*
> *He has done throughout the Bible and throughout my life.*

My belief in the I AM renewed, new facets of my testimony of belief began to take shape. My beloved Iron Rose Sisters, it is my fervent prayer that the I AM has and will reveal Himself to you in exactly the ways you need at the times you need it—He's great like that! So, what is your testimony of belief in the Great I AM?

Aha! There it is. The full title: **I *already* AM: Testimonies of Belief in the Great I AM.**

I pray that you can believe, as He revealed to me initially, "I *already* AM!"

And while you shouldn't believe simply because of my testimony, if God can use the testimonies of belief in this book, from Scripture and from other women in our lives, to invite you to know and believe in the I AM, then our mission has been accomplished.

As the Samaritans said to the woman who invited them to meet Jesus, *"It is no longer because of what you said that we believe, for we have heard for ourselves and know that this One is indeed the Savior of the world"* (John 4:42).

Now the question remains as John proposed it and Jesus Himself asked it, "Do you believe that I AM?"

CHAPTER 1

Fixing Our Eyes on the I AM

Jesus said to them, "Truly, truly, I say to you, before Abraham was, I am."
(John 8:58)

Can someone else be in charge? My sanity demands it.

Same song, tenth verse. The broken record rang in my ears as I lamented the current state of affairs. Others were tired of hearing it and I was tired of saying it!

Exhaustion from the weight of life's stresses clouded my thinking as I attempted to check something off my to-do list and seek a way out from under it. I had to find a solution!

A friend recommended the concept of uni-tasking: working on one thing at a time and a focused approach to that one task at hand before moving on to the next.

When I first heard this suggestion, I cringed at the prick to my pride. I *used* to pride myself on my multi-tasking. But my "expert" multi-tasking skills were failing me. And were they really worth bragging about?

I heard myself fall into the same trap of repetitive frustration and complaint. Others cringed on the other end of the phone as I broached the subject. Why did my words ring negative? Why were my inadequacies glaringly evident?

My prayers cried out in desperation to God. Desperate to get off the crazy train. Anxious to disembark the spinning carousel. My thoughts were my greater enemy than the daunting tasks at hand; the overwhelmed frustrations became mountains in my mind.

My rambling cries to God culminated in a myriad of questions, "Can someone else be in charge? I don't want to be responsible. Can I turn over the reins? Can someone tell me what to do next? How do I discern the priorities? Maybe it will all stop long enough for me to catch my breath..."

My questions continued in a torrent of words and emotions. And I came back to my initial question, "Can someone else be in charge?"

> *After a deep sigh, relieved to express my deepest longing to God, grateful for the ability to put it into words, He responded. A still small voice, a quieting of my spirit, a gentle embrace with a patient chuckle ushered me into the clear statement, "I already am. I AM."*

Did you catch that?! The Great I AM was already in charge of my life, of my situation, of my world—the same world that I felt was spinning out of control.

The One who was and is and is to come was already in charge, taking care of things in ways I could not comprehend. He's got this. I can let go. I should let go. I will let go. And let Him lead.

No matter what the questions you are asking, the problems you are facing, the doubts, fears, confusion, or frustration that clouds your mind, I invite you to hear the gentle, welcoming response of our eternal Father, "I *already* AM."

Your question may be expressed with different words. What is one of the questions you are facing in your own life?

What is your response to hearing "I *already* AM" from the Great I AM in the midst of your current life circumstances?

Even if you don't yet hear an answer, may we rest in the promise of the Great I AM and dwell in His presence today. He's already there. And He's got this. Whatever it is.

Let's Connect with the I AM Together

The I AM is the focus of this interactive Bible study book, but you are not on this journey alone. God has provided us with the opportunity to discover or rediscover who He is and learn from testimonies of belief in the I AM.

Each week, you will study the chapter on your own, and then gather with other sisters in Christ to connect with the I AM and with one another more deeply. The purpose of this book is to equip you in those relationships as we will have the opportunity to dig deeper into many of the names and qualities of God, together.

Throughout each chapter, some questions will be highlighted with the logo of Iron Rose Sister Ministries (IRSM).

A bilingual (English and Spanish) women's ministry resource, Iron Rose Sister Ministries is dedicated to equipping, encouraging, and empowering women in their relationships with God and other women. The name is rooted in the fact that we all want that kind of Christian sister who can serve as iron sharpening iron (Prov. 27:17), inspiring us to be as beautiful as a rose, in spite of a few thorns—an

Iron Rose Sister. For more information about the ministry and its resources, visit www.IronRoseSister.com

The IRSM logo also identifies questions you can use for good discussion when you meet with your small group (your Iron Rose Sisters). Here is the first suggested question for discussion in this chapter:

Which name of God, the I AM, most speaks to your current circumstance?

If you don't know a name of God that you can call on right now, that's okay! Thank you for committing not just to learn more about the I AM but, more importantly, to get to know Him personally and believe in Him. We will grow in our knowledge of and belief in the I AM, thus inspiring us to share who He is with others and to point them to the I AM.

From Moses to Me: Testimonies of Belief

Testimonies are powerful because they are stories. We learn from stories. We connect to stories. We identify with stories and find ourselves in them. Whether shared orally, read on the page of a book or the screen of a phone, as world-renowned Christian author C.S. Lewis said, "We read to know we are not alone."

Lewis is quoted as saying this in a movie about his life, entitled *Shadowlands*. A review of this movie by C.S. Lewis fans summarizes well one of the greatest tragedies, if we focus on the storyteller instead of on the I AM. "The great irony of *Shadowlands* is that it even as it draws people closer to Lewis, it may drive them further away from the One in whom Lewis found the meaning of life"[1].

Christ was the incarnation of the I AM—the Word who became flesh and dwelled among us—in order that we might have the living testimony of God on earth. We, individually and as the body of Christ, are invited to become the incarnation of Christ in the lives of others. Thus, our testimonies of belief, our stories, are living testimonies of the I AM on earth.

Jesus used stories (parables) as a way of pointing us to the Father and teaching us to see things from His perspective. Jesus learned His storytelling abilities from His Father, who narrated the entire Bible as a story revealing Himself as the I AM and making His Way clear. There is no greater testimony of who God is than the I AM in the flesh (God incarnate)! And those who were open to truly meeting the Messiah were drawn to Him, believed in Him, and found life in His name.

According to John 8:25-30, what is the result of hearing who Jesus is and who the Father is?

Getting Things in the Right Order

In the story found in John 8:25-30, we glimpse a summary of the motivation of John's gospel. Yet, John finally reveals the purpose of all he has written when he closes his gospel with his thesis statement. Most writers would put it at the beginning of their discourse. However, even evidenced by the placement of his thesis statement,

---

1 John West, "How Hollywood reinvented C.S. Lewis in the film "Shadowlands,"" last modified July 2, 2012, http://www.cslewisweb.com/2012/07/how-hollywood-reinvented-c-s-lewis-in-the-film-shadowlands/

John emphasizes the priorities of highest importance and the order in which we should look at things ourselves.

Read John 20:30-31 and list John's two reasons for sharing his testimony and writing his account.

With John 20:30-31 in mind, why did John end his gospel with this statement instead of beginning with it? What did he emphasize first in his book overall? (Feel free to refer back to John chapter 1 and skim through the gospel in order to conceptualize this from a big picture perspective.)

> *John, more than any other biblical writer, focuses on the identity of God as the key to belief and the abundant life.*

We cannot allow these things to get out of order in our priorities.

Fixing Our Eyes on the I AM

At Iron Rose Sister Ministries, we strive to equip women to focus on the I AM and, in turn, help others do the same—connecting to God and one another more deeply. The beauty of the diversity of our Iron Rose Sisters is that we do not all see things in the same way. When we share our insights and perspectives, we learn a little more about the I AM and are invited to encounter other facets of who He is.

We will spend many of the chapters of this book delving into various passages of John and Jesus' self-proclamations as the I AM.

However, our goal of getting to know the I AM and believing in His name will not be limited to that gospel.

What stories (outside the book of John) come to mind of those who truly came to know the I AM and showed who He was to others?

Many of the people that come to my mind are mentioned among the heroes of the faith listed in Hebrews 11. They each encountered different aspects of the I AM, even if they never saw the fulfillment of all that was promised (Heb. 11:39-40).

They are not spectators in our race; they are witnesses (Heb. 12:1). Their stories are testimonies of belief and examples of how to maintain our focus. With them in our cloud of witnesses, among countless others today, what does Hebrews 12:1-2 say should be our focused goals?

Why is it important to keep our eyes fixed on Jesus throughout the journey?

What happens when we lose sight of Jesus? Are any other life goals possible?

Seeing is Believing from the I AM's Perspective

The illustration is made of five blind Chinese men who were asked to describe an elephant.

The first man stepped up to the elephant, felt with his hands, smelled with his nose and said, "It is long and narrow, very flexible, like a snake, but with a little brush on the end. It is also very stinky."

"Long and narrow?" responded the second man. "It is more like a thick hose that, ay! Sprays out the end!"

"It is no hose at all," said the third man, the shortest of the five. "It is most like a tree, rough and solid. Much thicker than a hose."

"If my friend declared it a tree," interjected the fourth man. "I most definitely have the biggest leaf I have ever encountered. It is thin and waves in the wind."

"No. You all have it wrong. It is broad and wide, like a wall," concluded the fifth man.

Which man was correct? And which man was wrong?

How does God see the elephant?

How are we like the blind men?

Only God has the clear perspective of the big picture. Only God is able to address the whole elephant. What we are dealing with... our questions in life... They are barely a wrinkle on the elephant's knee.

Reflection: Am I trusting the I AM with the whole elephant?

We will be looking through the lens of the I AM because **it matters not what the world says, but rather what the Word says.**

And when I keep my eyes fixed on the I AM, when I strive to see things from His perspective, I avoid the trap of the futile searches for answers, identity, purpose, provision, or whatever else I am seeking. **Because everything else falls short of the I AM.**

Focusing on the I AM and Not What He Answers

When we get lost in the search for what we should do with our part of the elephant, we have lost sight of the I AM who has the eternal perspective. We are called to believe in Him, trust His plan, and call on His name (John 3:16; John 14:1; Rom. 10:9). The focus cannot be on ourselves.

Questions about identity and purpose pervade our culture and consume our thoughts. We seek answers in all the wrong places and **the focus itself is in error when we make it more about ME than HE who designed our identity and dictates our purpose.**

If one were able to give us all the answers, even as God reveals them in Scripture, our focus would be mistaken. Are we seeking answers or the Answer?

Refer back to the "life question" you wrote down in answer to the very first question in this chapter (pg. 8). If your motivation for reading this book is to answer that initial question, put this book away. Don't finish it. Your question may not get answered—at least not in the way you hope.

However, if your motivation is to deepen your relationship with the I AM and strengthen your belief in Him, your *true* questions *will* be answered through an increasingly powerful testimony of belief in the I AM.

Through this book, you won't be "won over" or convinced by the perfect answer to the perfect question, rather you will be more thoroughly equipped to know and believe in the I AM. Here's an expression that summarizes this thought:

"What you win them with is what you win them to"

During my four years at Harding University, I worked as a student assistant for Dr. Daniel Stockstill, a family friend and respected professor in the College of Bible and Religion. By grading his students' papers and reviewing their notes from his classes, I essentially audited the Youth Ministry and Old Testament Survey classes he taught. Many of the lessons seeped into the back of my mind, later to be referenced when working in various ministry contexts.

One specific, significant phrase was, "What you win them with is what you win them to."

Take a moment to re-read and reflect on that expression. "What you win them WITH is what you win them TO." Here is an example: You invite some friends to church because the preacher is awesome, or the worship is impactful. What happens when that preacher moves away or when the songs led on a particular Sunday are not your friend's favorite? You have "won them" with some of the secondary benefits and blessings rather than winning them to Christ.

Now, name two more examples of "What you win them with is what you win them to," in a church or Christian context, how it applies to this book, or in another area of life.

Unfortunately, this expression applied to my initial efforts and creative process in writing this book, as referenced in the Introduction and affirmed through my own answers to the Common Threads below. Thankfully, the I AM doesn't give up on us in our transformation process—thus strengthening our testimony of belief in Him.

Common Threads

We will close this chapter with an introduction to the Common Threads. They are represented by the three parts of the Iron Rose Sister Ministries logo and are a tool for personal and practical application of a lesson. As such, they are utilized in each chapter of all Iron Rose Sister Ministries interactive Bible study books. They also offer the opportunity to pray over each other in a small group setting regarding spiritual matters.

The Common Threads are also an exercise through which you can grow in your spiritual friendships as Iron Rose Sisters—to be that "iron sharpening iron" (Prov. 27:17) as we encourage and inspire one another to be as beautiful as a rose, in spite of a few thorns. By walking on this journey of belief in the I AM together with other Christian women, I invite you to learn what it really means to have an accountability partner, a prayer partner, and a Christian friend: An Iron Rose Sister.

Each person's answer will be distinct as the I AM meets us where we are and invites us into a greater testimony of belief. Sometimes, while working on the chapter alone, your response to the Common Threads will be obvious. At other times, the discussion of the chapter with your Iron Rose Sisters will make your responses more evident.

Don't forget to make note of the date at the end of the chapter as a form of spiritual journaling. Your own notes become a testimony of belief in the I AM!

The specific application of the Common Threads for this book can be phrased as they are listed below, first with my own answers. Sometimes they will appear together at the end of a chapter. In other chapters, they will be interspersed throughout the chapter, but will be recognizable by the three parts of the logo.

Michelle's Common Threads This Week

In reference to my personal story in the Introduction and the one from the beginning of this chapter, I would like to share with you my Common Threads for this week's lesson and some of my personal goals for the entire book:

A name or characteristic of the I AM that I will **grow and bloom** in my belief of:

The I AM, the Sovereign Lord—the One who is in charge, not me.

Removing the **thorn** of a flawed perspective or distracted focus:

A dependence on my own abilities and the pride of trying to do what is God's job to do.

Ways in which an Iron Rose Sister can serve as **iron sharpening iron** and encourage me to **dig deeper** in my relationship with the I AM:

Remind me of my commitment to look first to the I AM and point others to Him. (Even throughout this book, I invite you to keep me accountable.)

A verse, word of encouragement, or reminder of the I AM:

John 8:58, "Truly, truly, I say to you, before Abraham was born, I AM!" [emphasis mine]

Common Threads

Now, it's your turn!

A name or characteristic of the I AM that you will **grow and bloom** in your belief of:

Removing the **thorn** of a flawed perspective or distracted focus:

Ways in which an Iron Rose Sister can serve as **iron sharpening iron** and encourage you to **dig deeper** in your relationship with the I AM:

A verse, word of encouragement, or reminder of the I AM:

Thank you for joining with me and other Iron Rose Sisters on a journey of clearer focus and deeper belief in the I AM. We can't wait to hear your testimony of belief!

Date of completion: _____

CHAPTER 2

The Great I AM: Who Was and Is and Is to Come

"I am the Alpha and the Omega," says the Lord God, "who is and who was and who is to come, the Almighty." (Rev. 1:8)

Moses was one of the first to whom the I AM revealed Himself. Beginning with a miraculous birth (since all the other Hebrew baby boys were being killed, Ex. 1:16), it was clear Moses was put on earth for a purpose. And he knew it too!

"I was no ordinary child. From an early age, everyone knew I was special. To start with, I was the only kid in my grade—the only Hebrew kid, that is.

My Hebrew roots were obvious because of how I looked, but I was safe in Pharaoh's house, raised by his daughter. The God of my fathers had been merciful.

Even though the king had ordered that all the newborn boys be killed, my mom sent me down the river in a basket and Pharaoh's daughter rescued me. My sister, Miriam, was watching nearby, just as she always was looking after me. Then, at Miriam's suggestion, mom was able to nurse me and tell me stories of the God of Abraham, Isaac and Jacob, even while living in the Egyptian palace.

The stories of the Hebrew God intermingled with the education and wisdom of the Egyptians by whom I was trained.

My life was easy and blessed. **I was "powerful in speech and action"** (Acts 7:22), *but I knew the pain and oppression of my people, the Israelites. So, when I was about forty, I was ready. I had known my whole life that I was saved for a special purpose—to save God's people. And I was ready to step up and fulfill my calling.* **"I've got this," I thought.**

So when I decided to visit my own people, and saw one of them being mistreated by an Egyptian, I went to his defense and killed the Egyptian.

I was sure that by avenging that Israelite, the people would realize that our God was using me to rescue them (Acts 7:25). However, that was not how it played out.

The next day, some Israelites were fighting, and I tried to step in, but what I had done the day before backfired on me and my leadership was rejected.

Dejected and discouraged, I fled to Midian where I settled as a foreigner, married, and had two sons. I stayed in Midian forty years, mostly working as a shepherd, which gave me a lot of time to reflect on what I had done and how I had mishandled things."

Moses Meets the I AM

For this week's lesson, we pick up at this point in the story, beginning in Exodus 3. Moses is about eighty years old and is still living in Midian. He knew about the Hebrew God but had run from Him and did not know Him personally... yet. Like other Israelites, he might have wondered if his cries were being heard.

Read Exodus 3 once to get the flow of the story, then read back through chapter 3, answering the following questions:

What did Moses see and why did he go over to look (Exodus 3:2-3)?

What did God say about the place where Moses was standing? And what is the significance of it being what God called it (Ex. 3:5)?

Who does God say He is in Exodus 3:6? And how does Moses react?

Why do you think Moses reacted that way (Exodus 3:6)?

What do we learn about God from His interaction with Moses in the first six verses of Exodus 3?

One of the things that has always been interesting to me is the fact that God did not reveal Himself, nor His identity or purpose, until Moses came over to look (Ex. 3:3-4). Why do you think God was waiting for Moses to take the initiative?

Continuing in Exodus 3:7-8, we learn aspects of God's eternal nature: who He is and what He does.

> [7] Then the LORD said, "I have surely seen the affliction of my people who are in Egypt and have heard their cry because of their taskmasters. I know their sufferings, [8] and I have come down to deliver them out of the hand of the Egyptians and to bring them up out of that land to a good and broad land, a land flowing with milk and honey, to the place of the Canaanites, the Hittites, the Amorites, the Perizzites, the Hivites, and the Jebusites.

Make a list of the five verb phrases that reveal who God is or what He does from these two verses (Hint: In verse 8, the "coming down" has two purposes/verb phrases).

Have those five characteristics of God changed? _____ Do you truly believe that? _____

The God who was and is and is to come saw, heard, knew, delivered, and provided for the Israelites. Jesus, in the flesh, saw, heard, knew, delivered, and provided in ways that people could tangibly experience. The I AM, today, still sees, hears, knows, delivers, and provides! And our Heavenly Father, for all eternity, will see, hear, know, deliver, and provide. Amen!

How have you experienced God seeing, hearing, knowing, delivering or providing? (Feel free to write out the story on separate paper or in the Notes/Testimonies section at the back of the book. And when sharing your story in the small group context with your Iron Rose Sisters, you can choose which highlights to share, and make a plan to get coffee with a few of the women to share the full version of each of your God stories later, as well!)

Moses' Next Steps with the I AM

Your answer about how you have experienced God is part of your testimony of belief. And, like Moses, God has something for you to do with that testimony, even beyond sharing it with your Iron Rose Sisters over a cup of coffee.

After what God clarifies in Exodus 3:7-9, what does that mean for Moses in verse 10?

Why is it significant that God waits to give Moses his purpose until after establishing His own identity (Ex. 3:6) and stating His own purpose (Ex. 3:7-9)?

What do you think was going through Moses' mind when he asks his question in Exodus 3:11? Think about what was happening in that moment, but also knowing his history and past experiences.

How does God respond in Exodus 3:12? Does God actually answer Moses' question? How so or how not?

Who Do I Tell Them Sent Me?

After Moses begins to accept his assignment, he asks, *"If I come to the people of Israel and say to them, 'The God of your fathers has sent me to you,' and they ask me, 'What is his name?' what shall I say to them?"* (Ex. 3:13).

Write out verses 14 and 15 of Exodus 3. Pay special attention to which words and letters are capitalized.

Throughout the book of Genesis, we see God slowly reveal Himself to His chosen people. He becomes known as the God of Abraham, Isaac, and Jacob, but, as of yet, He is not known by a specific name. (In the next lessons, we will explore more of what I AM means in the original language and for us today, as declared by the I AM Himself.)

Another way in which the I AM affirms His identity and His purpose is through promises of accompaniment (Ex. 3:12) and provision (Ex. 3:21-22). Where do we see the same promises in other passages of the Bible?

Is there anything else we learn about God from Exodus chapter 3?

Doubts and Fears

Now let's continue with Exodus 4. We will follow a similar pattern of study as we did in Exodus 3: Read the entire chapter, then we will answer some questions.

How does Exodus 4 begin? What is going on in Moses' mind?

After God's patient affirmations and signs for Moses in Exodus 4:2-9, what happens in verse 10?

How does God react to Moses' excuses?

Who else does God respond to in a similar way (other stories in the Bible)?

The irony in Exodus 4:14 is that God offers Moses support, even after being angry and frustrated with him. What does this teach us about God's character?

Following the rest of the story in Exodus 4, we see that God used Moses and Aaron as His instruments through which others came to know the I AM. Their testimony of belief became an invitation... *"And the people believed..."* (Ex. 4:31).

However, their belief often wavered, sometimes because of forgetfulness or distraction or doubt. Yet God, in His great mercy, reiterated His promise of deliverance time and time again, often revealed through His different names. We see this with Moses and the Israelites a few chapters later (Ex. 6:1-12) and the story repeats throughout the Bible and in our own lives! What a blessing to be able to call on the various names of God as a reminder of His promises and provision!

The "Many Sides" of God

During a holiday visit, my niece (who was three at the time) had chosen our assigned seats at the table in order to sit next to me, "Aunt M," at every meal. Her older brother was ready to have a turn to sit with Aunt M, so he planted himself in "her chair" for the evening meal.

My sister affirmed the fairness of allowing my nephew to have a turn, but my niece was not happy with this change. Wisely seeking a compromise, and already beginning to shift some of the chairs around the table, my sister said, "I have an idea," and asked her daughter, "How many sides does Aunt M have?"

Pausing to contemplate her answer, then with a pensive look on her face, my niece proudly replied, "Many sides."

Surprised by her response and humored by the truth she expressed, we each were left with the reflection of our limited perspective of the two sides on which my nephew and niece could sit. Unable to refrain from chuckling, I quickly responded, "You are absolutely right, Zeni. Aunt M has many sides."

Zeni was 100% correct. I am not a box that has sides. I am not even a circle that is endless, although "round" is a better description than square.

A three-year-old's perspective of my "many sides" inspired a child-like faith in the limitless sides of the I AM.

> *The I AM is infinite in His qualities, eternal in His nature.*

What happens when we put God in a box and limit His "many sides"?

Hardships in life, doubts, fears, and our own limitations put a strain on our faith because we are focused on ourselves. We lose sight of God. And when our belief staggers, we limit the I AM.

In contrast, what happens when we expand our thinking and allow God to be all that He *already* is as the I AM, who was and is and is to come?

The Limitless God

Name three things we use to limit God (e.g. time).

God's existence supersedes any of the obstacles or limitations we put on Him.

> *The I AM is in ALL, above ALL, beyond ALL,*
> *through ALL; He IS ALL—the I AM.*

His very existence, as we will affirm in other chapters, is all-present (omnipresent, Ps. 139:7-12), all-knowing (omniscient, Ps. 139:1-6), and all-powerful (omnipotent, Ps. 147:4-5). Each of these eternal qualities are ones on which we can depend, rely, and believe with certainty.

What do we learn from the following passages about the I AM?

Malachi 3:6/James 1:17

Hebrews 13:8

What does it mean if God never changes?

Why do we sometimes think that God has changed? What is it that has really changed? (Hint: It's not God!)

What happens in my life when I believe the I AM never changes?

List the names and descriptions of the I AM and His eternal nature from the following verses in Revelation.

Revelation 1:8, 17

Revelation 21:6

Revelation 22:13

Alpha and Omega, First and Last, Beginning and End

When facing a new beginning, we have no idea what the end will look like. We can dream of what we hope it becomes. We can plan and set goals toward what we deem an attainable end.

However, unexpected things will happen along the way. We are not in control. Change is a constant. And interruptions are always possible.

Yet, God is not surprised by any of these detours. For Him, they are not detours. Instead, they are part of the story and part of the journey.

God is the Alpha and the Omega, the First and the Last, the Beginning and the End (Rev. 22:13). He goes before us, behind us, and surrounds us (Ps. 125:2).

God is the source of life and the conqueror of death (1 Cor. 15:55). He is the Root and the Offspring of David (Rev. 22:16).

He who was and is and is to come, the eternal, cannot be caught off guard.

> *The Alpha and the Omega are the first and last letters of the Greek alphabet. The I AM is the Author of everything.*
>
> *The First and the Last imply there is an order to things. The I AM is in control of everything.*
>
> *The Beginning and the End illustrate a timeframe. The I AM, Creator, knows when and how everything will happen.*

What a comfort to believe in the I AM, the One who always was, always is and always will be!

Take a moment to reflect on what it means that God not only was there in the beginning, but that He is the beginning. Without His existence nothing existed, exists, or will exist.

Reflection: When I contemplate the eternal nature of God, does it make it easier to trust the I AM with every aspect of my life?

Trusting the I AM's Authority and Timing

Part of Moses' journey to belief was an invitation to trust...

Returning to Exodus 3 and 4, what does the I AM demonstrate authority over?

Does the I AM still have authority over those same things today? Give some examples.

According to 2 Peter 3:8-9, how does God see time?

As highlighted by Moses' story at the beginning of this chapter, it was not when Moses felt ready, strong of speech and action, that God used him (see Acts 7:20-38). He had failed to trust God's timing. Does anyone other than me identify with these trust issues?

If we were to interview Moses and ask him to tell us some of the rest of his story, I think it might've gone something like this:

I learned quite a few things throughout my encounters with the I AM, since first meeting Him in the burning bush:

➢ *God had a plan for my life, but I had taken it into my own hands and was trying to make it happen in my way and in my timing (what happened in Egypt at age 40).*

> ➢ God didn't use me when I was young, "powerful of speech and action," but rather when I was older, more humble, and stuttered. Ask any other 80-year-old; age has a way of humbling you.

> ➢ God waited until I let go of trying to control how He saved His people, so that I could be used simply as an instrument in His hands. I was honored to be a part of foreshadowing the concepts of rescue and redemption to be fulfilled later when the I AM became flesh.

If only I had continued to believe that I AM knew what was best and was truly in control. Unfortunately, I always struggled with taking matters back into my own hands, especially when the people grumbled and complained.

And I paid a bitter price for not leaving it in God's hands and not trusting Him and His plan. I struck the rock twice instead of speaking to it (Num. 20:1-14). By taking it in my own hands, I rejected God and was unable to enter the Promised Land.

While I never stepped foot into the promised land of Canaan, God's grace is great and I do, now, taste the profound goodness of God in the eternal Promised Land.

I hope that others can learn from my mistakes and my testimony of belief... May you fully trust in the I AM, who was and is and is to come.

 What have you learned from your encounters with the I AM? How do you think your answers would change at different points of your life? Imagine yourself answering those questions at age 20, 40, and 80.

It is humbling to realize that as much as our understanding of the I AM changes over time, He does not. Jesus, the I AM incarnate, is the same yesterday, today, and forever. The I AM is the One who was and is and is to come. **Our perspective is limited. Our God is limitless.**

As we grow and deepen our belief in the I AM, may we trust and see things from the eternal, limitless perspective of the I AM. As Moses learned, God's way is best, and He always knows what He is talking about.

Common Threads

The Common Threads for this week may come from a reflection on Moses' life or the eternal nature of the I AM. It may also come from something else that God has put on your heart or in your mind as you walk with Him.

You may feel vulnerable putting these things on paper, but the I AM already knows. He longs for us to come to Him with the doubts and fears. And just as He did with Moses, and many others whose testimonies of belief we will share, God is patient to answer us and remind us of His truths—especially His promises that He will be with us. **Remember? The I AM is the One who was and is and is to come. He's not going anywhere—and that Truth has not changed!**

He has also provided Iron Rose Sisters with whom you share this journey of deeper belief in the I AM. Satan wants to isolate us and make us think we are alone in our struggles or doubts. However, when we bring them to light, the accuser loses his power over us and the eternal Light of the I AM gives us hope and comfort.

A name or characteristic of the I AM that you will **grow and bloom** in your belief of:

Removing the **thorn** of a flawed perspective or distracted focus:

Ways in which an Iron Rose Sister can serve as **iron sharpening iron** and encourage you to **dig deeper** in your relationship with the I AM:

A verse, word of encouragement, or reminder of the I AM:

Additional Exercise: You can also use the Common Threads as a way of processing how Moses would've responded at different points in his life. What would he have wanted to grow or bloom in? What was his thorn? Did he ever need reminders of the I AM from others that served as iron sharpening iron in his life?

Date of completion: _____

CHAPTER 3

Not "who am I?" but Who the I AM is.

God said to Moses, "I am who I am." And he said, "Say this to the people of Israel: 'I am has sent me to you.'" God also said to Moses, "Say this to the people of Israel: 'The LORD, the God of your fathers, the God of Abraham, the God of Isaac, and the God of Jacob, has sent me to you.' This is my name forever, and thus I am to be remembered throughout all generations. (Ex. 3:14-15)

Reading the title of this chapter may cause you to think that I am either a clever author or an incompetent one. I cannot take credit for the ingenuity of such a play on words. God, in His very name and nature, defies the rules of grammar and surpasses our understanding of the world as we try to comprehend it.

My friend Katie tells the story of when her oldest daughter was about five years old. "Mommy, I know about Jesus and I know about God. Who's the Lord?" Katie laughed and said, "Go ask your daddy!" Later, she did take the time to explain some of the names and characteristics of God to her inquisitive daughter. These concepts can be difficult to comprehend no matter what your age or level of study.

If you feel overwhelmed by the incomprehensible nature of our eternal God, may it be an awe-inspiring discovery and not a source of frustration. The I AM is neither an illusion nor a mirage. The fact that we cannot completely wrap our minds around the I AM is part of the wonderful mystery that is being revealed. Personally, I am grateful that He is beyond my comprehension. It is what makes Him God!

For my thoughts are not your thoughts, neither are your ways my ways, declares the LORD. *For as the heavens are higher than the earth, so are my ways higher than your ways and my thoughts than your thoughts.* (Is. 55:8-9)

As we get to know the I AM and strive to fix our eyes on Him, it is worthwhile to gain a basic understanding of His name and its origin because of what they reveal.

Language of the Time

My study of the I AM has taken me on a novice-level dive into the linguistic worlds of Hebrew and Greek in order to better capture the meaning of God's name. Tempting as it is to get into my nerdy linguistic passion and extend this section into an entire book, I promise to limit our discovery of God's name to the facets of the I AM that are relevant to our study.

Language reveals nuances about culture and context. Words are the lens through which we gain understanding. Even when we don't speak the same language, we look for clues that bring us connection and community—universal truths that are common to all people. And through His name, God reveals who the I AM is in a way that illuminates many of the universal, amazing truths that transcend any cultural, linguistic, temporal, or other limitations.

Here are a few facts to keep in mind about the languages of the time:

➢ The Old Testament was written primarily in Hebrew with a few small portions in Aramaic.

> ➢ The New Testament was written in koine (commoner) Greek.

> ➢ The Greek translation of the Old Testament is called the Septuagint (or LXX because of the tradition that 70 or 72 Hebrew scholars dedicated themselves to the integrity of the translation). It was written in the 2nd or 3rd century B.C. It is quoted extensively throughout the New Testament.

> ➢ As the Son of God, we know He could speak whatever language He chose! However, Aramaic is likely the primary language Jesus would have spoken in the home. It is commonly believed that He would have read and spoken Hebrew (the scholarly language), as well as at least basic Greek (the most "universal" language of the Roman Empire, which ruled at that time, and was used in commerce). And perhaps even Latin since His boyhood town of Nazareth was near a major Roman city, Tiberias.

These references to the languages of the time will allow us to gain a more profound understanding of the meaning behind the names and descriptions referenced throughout Scripture.

The Hebrew "I AM"

Sometimes one language expresses a concept better than another language. And not every language is structured the same. **One special aspect of Hebrew is that God's proper name could not and should not ever be pronounced.**

The Hebrew language does not have "vowels," as we traditionally think of them (a, e, i, o, u). Rather, consonants are the foundation of the words. The majority of the Hebrew words are built from a three-consonant root. Vowels, voice, and derived stems (no tenses), are reflected by diacritics (small markings above and below the letters). One example of diacritics are the accent marks used in Spanish to designate which syllable is stressed in pronunciation: "término" and "terminó" are pronounced differently and mean different things ("term" and "he finished"). But, back to the Hebrew...

Look at Moses' name below and notice the dots above and below the three consonant characters. They are the "vowel" indications and therefore tell you how to pronounce the word, *Mosheh*.

מֹשֶׁה

Moses

יהוה

The second image is of the four consonants of God's name "YHWH," also known as the Tetragrammaton (meaning four letters). It has no vowel indications or diacritic markings, so there was no way to know today how it was to be pronounced. And the Jews never even tried to pronounce His name out of reverence.

YHWH is the Proper Name for God. Its root is the Hebrew verb *hayah or havah*, which both have the same consonant root, meaning "to be, become, fall out, come to pass, exist."

But with YHWH, we are talking about eternal existence, complete being. Without Him, life would cease to exist, nothing else could be or become. And in the same way that the Hebrew language does not reflect tense or time, the I AM is not limited by time.

Since the Hebrew root of I AM's name *YHWH* is the verb "to be or to exist," we can "simply" say that He is—always is, has been and will be.

The eternal I AM has planted eternity in our hearts, which is part of why we long for the eternal (Ecc. 3:11).

> *The incomprehensibility of His name reflects the limitless nature of His very existence—unencumbered by time, space, or any other dimension we use to define things.*

That is why when *YHWH* is translated into English, we see variations on "I AM who I AM" or "I WILL BE who I WILL BE" (Ex. 3:14-15).

Also an English accommodation, the name *Yahweh* or *Jehovah* comes from combining the Hebrew consonants for God's proper name *YHWH* and the vowels from *Adonai*, which means master, owner, or lord. *Adonai*, translated Lord (with only the L capitalized), is in contrast to LORD, which is the modern translation or representation of *YHWH* or the I AM.

Here is an example from Psalm 8:1.

> O LORD, *our Lord, how majestic is your name in all the earth! You have set your glory above the heavens.*

Notice the all CAPS in LORD (*Yahweh*), versus Lord (*Adonai*), even if the letters "ORD" are smaller than the L. One can think of the proper name "LORD" as a parallel of the Tetragrammaton (the "four letters" YHWH). It means so much more than what the four letters represent!

Thanks for sticking with me through this short lesson on the Hebrew origin of God's name! Take a breath, stretch your legs, take a moment and let it soak in! Feel free to go back and read it again, or as many times as you want. It has taken me years to try and wrap my head around these concepts and I still have so much to learn! You can use this as a reference in the future; and we will explore more of the application of these concepts through the other chapters.

The Greek "I AM"

You may also be saying, as the Greeks themselves say in jest to Americans who visit their country, "It's all Greek to me!" Yet we will simplify the Greek aspect of our discovery of the I AM, so bear with me a bit longer. There are a few more amazing truths to reveal about the I AM, YHWH, Yahweh, Jehovah, LORD.

Here is what you need to know:

➢ I AM or YHWH from the Hebrew was most often translated "*egō eimi*" in the Septuagint (Greek translation of the Old Testament).

➢ The same phrasing was used by Jesus, as quoted by John, "*egō eimi.*"

➢ The use of the same phrasing was a proclamation of equality with YHWH by Jesus, a blasphemous statement in the ears of the Jewish leaders.

➢ There are definite parallels in origin, meaning, name, title, and function between the following:

  o I AM (Old Testament and New Testament)

  o YHWH (Hebrew transliterated into English characters)

  o egō eimi (Greek transliterated into English characters)

  o Yahweh

  o LORD (not "Lord")

  o Jehovah (least preferred because it is furthest from the original translation)

Therefore, when we look at the names of God which describe His functions, roles, or manifestations, **at the essence and root of each of**

His characteristics is His eternal Presence, His being—the One who was and is and is to come—The Existence—The Life—The I AM.

> What have you learned about the I AM, YHWH, Yahweh, Jehovah, LORD from a brief lesson on the Hebrew and Greek languages as they relate to God's name?

> From the Common Threads: What is a name or characteristic of the I AM that you will **grow and bloom** in your belief of?

"Who am I?" versus Who the I AM is

Did you notice the Greek way to say, "I AM"? *Egō eimi.* Does that first word look familiar?

"Ego"... "I"... But which "I" is it all about?

The trap of making it all about oneself is an easy one to fall into. The accuser, Satan, is crafty in his efforts to trip us up in whatever way he can. From Eve to the end of the Revelation story, we see him at work.

> What specific Bible stories come to mind in which Satan tempted someone with a focus on "self" rather than on God?

How does Satan try to distract us with a focus on "self" today?

What happens when the I AM reveals Himself in those Bible stories or in the stories of our own lives?

We love when the I AM reveals Himself in ways that only He can! Those God stories are powerful testimonies of belief that give I AM all the glory.

Like Shadrach, Meshach, and Abednego...

> *Our belief cannot be dependent on the I AM showing up in the way we want or when we want.*

Besides, the I AM is already there... "I *already* AM."

> [16] *Shadrach, Meshach and Abednego replied to him, "King Nebuchadnezzar, we do not need to defend ourselves before you in this matter.* [17] *If we are thrown into the blazing furnace, the God we serve is able to deliver us from it, and he will deliver us from Your Majesty's hand.* [18] ***But even if he does not**, we want you to know, Your Majesty, that we will not serve your gods or worship the image of gold you have set up."* (Dan. 3:16-18, NIV, emphasis mine)

It's Not About You Anyway

Evidenced in the stories already told on myself, one can easily fall into the trap of focusing on self. When God gently reminded me that "I AM, I *already* AM" is in charge, I realized that I had lost the

I ALREADY AM • 45

perspective of who the I AM was or what He could do through me—even more significantly—what He could do without me. None of it was dependent on me. "I *already* AM" was in control. Little ole "I" was not.

Reminds me of another woman who needed a reminder of Who it was all about (hint: It wasn't her!). Mordecai told Esther,

> "For if you keep silent at this time, relief and deliverance will rise for the Jews from another place, but you and your father's house will perish. And who knows whether you have not come to the kingdom for such a time as this?" (Esther 4:14)

In other words, when Esther wanted to say I can't do it, **Mordecai reminded her that the I AM can and will, even if you don't choose to let Him use you. It is not about you anyway!** God is so much bigger than that (Eph. 3:20-21)!

| I can't. | I AM can, will, and already did. |
| I am not _____ enough. | I AM *already* is enough. |

Esther was focused on her fears, her inadequacies, her thorns, herself...

From the Common Threads: What **thorn** in your own life needs to be removed from your focus?

From Extraordinary to Ordinary

Job had also lost his perspective on who the I AM was. As you possibly mentioned in answer to the earlier question about those the accuser attacked, Satan was especially evil in his schemes with Job.

Turn with me to the book of Job as we explore Job's testimony of belief as a final example for this chapter: how the I AM reveals

Himself in the midst of Job's circumstances. Read Job 1 and refresh your memory about his story.

What made Job an extraordinary person (Job 1:1-8)?

Satan saw how extraordinary Job was and did not like it! He proposed that Job's fear of God and avoidance of evil was only because of God's blessings in his life. Another way of phrasing the accusation from the accuser is, "Sure Job worships you. You gave him an extraordinary life. But can I make him ordinary and see if he still thinks you're all that?"

Even as Job's wealth was taken away and his children were stripped out of his hands (Job 1:13-19), Job did not, as his wife urged, "curse God or die." **Job chose to let God remain the extraordinary one.** Wow! What a testimony of belief!

How does Job refer to God in Job 1:21? Pay special attention to capital vs. lower case letters.

After the adversary (Satan) attacks Job's health, how does Job respond to his wife in Job 2:10?

The name Job uses to refer to God in Job 2:10 is the Hebrew *Elohim*. It is actually the first word or first name we see used to describe God in Genesis. It means Almighty or all-powerful—apt for the Creator of the heavens and the earth, right?

What is in a Name?

Even though *Elohim*/Almighty is His eternal characteristic, it is not His name. I am a sister, an aunt, a daughter, outgoing, verbal... but none of those is my name, Michelle.

Rose is not my name although many people call me "Rose" because of the name of Iron Rose Sister Ministries. This gets even funnier in Spanish, but we will save that story for another time... There is no need to correct them because, while it is not my proper name, "Rose" is still a characteristic I hope to embody—being as beautiful as a rose, in spite of a few thorns.

Elohim is a characteristic or description. "I AM Who I AM" or "I WILL BE Who I WILL BE" is His proper name. Once someone has a name, we can relate to them and learn more about them. And so, even though Almighty is His eternal characteristic, it is not His name. YHWH or LORD is. **And at the moment of Job's suffering, Job transitions from YHWH or the I AM being present with him to feeling the distance of what *Elohim*, the Almighty's character has allowed to happen.**

> *Job doesn't understand, but he chooses to trust and believe, even when he feels alone.*

The I AM was present with Job in his grief even though YHWH may not have been physically present with shoulders to cry on or hands to hold. He did not leave nor forsake Job (Job 23:8-10), which are the same promises we have today (Matt. 28:18-20). We have His Spirit dwelling in those of us who believe and have been born again into the new life through Him (Acts 2:38)! Not only is that a blessing for us directly, it is also a blessing to others when our presence represents the I AM's Presence in their lives (2 Cor. 3:3).

Radical Human Presence versus Cheap Words

How did Job's friends respond to Job's situation in Job 2:11-13?

We can serve as incarnations or representatives of the I AM's Presence in the lives of others (2 Cor. 3:18). It is when we open our mouths, like Job's friends did, that we fall short.

Job and his friends spend the next 34 chapters expressing their frustrations, grief, questions, confusion, doubts, and disbelief.

Through the discourses from Job's friends, we see that they wanted Job to focus on what they thought he had done wrong in order to rectify his situation. They neglected to trust in the I AM who was already there and had things under control.

From the Common Threads: What are ways in which an Iron Rose Sister can serve as **iron sharpening iron** and encourage you to **dig deeper** in your relationship with the I AM, especially during difficult times? (Job's friends may or may not be the best example...)

The I AM Makes His Presence Known

After Job's wife and friends express their perspective and advice for Job, God steps in and clears things up. The I AM was there all along—always has been and always will be. Job had lost sight of the LORD through his circumstances. **His questions focused more on**

"who am I that this would happen to me?" than Who the I AM *already* is, no matter the circumstances. Job's grief was real and valid, but Job had lost his focus on YHWH.

The I AM makes His Presence known and clarifies the manifestations of His Presence through the questions He asks Job. Write out three of the questions God asks Job from chapters 38-41 in the book of Job.

In the same way that God did not answer Moses' question of "how?", God does not answer Job's questions of "why?". The answer is always "I AM."

What facets of the I AM's character did Job need to be reminded of?

The I AM is Present, Right Where We Are—Believe It!

"Father" is one of the primary characteristics of God I have clung to at different points of my life to remind me of the One in whom I believe. "Father" is who I often look to and want to point others to. I used to say that I love to "Meet someone where they are and walk with them one step closer to the Father." **However, other eternal qualities of the I AM may speak to someone's current circumstance in a more powerful and present way.**

I AM, YHWH, Yahweh, Jehovah, LORD makes His Presence known by His very Being. His name means "being," and you don't get more "present" than that. He even gave up all His glory to become physically present with us (Phil. 2:5-11). **And remember: Present is not just a time thing. He who was and is and is to come, Alpha and Omega, First and Last, Beginning and End has got this.** Present through all time and in all places. Amen!

Therefore, as my understanding of the I AM has grown, I now say that I want to join with the I AM in meeting someone where they are and walking with them both, together.

YHWH's name is an invitation to be there with Him. God steps in and says, "I *already* AM... I AM" and makes Himself known in powerful and humbling ways. He meets us where we are and draws us to Him.

A Final Prayer of Belief

Through this week's lesson, it is my fervent prayer that you have been blessed by an understanding of the I AM's name and by the gentle reminder of the YHWH's Presence, as revealed by His very name. In exploring other aspects of His character, may we never lose sight of His name as the foundation and root of His "Being" each of those other titles and descriptors.

> *The I AM, YHWH, Yahweh, Jehovah, LORD—the One in whom we believe—invites you to believe in the manifestations and incarnations of His existence and to share your testimonies of belief with others.*

Let's look to the I AM (His name affirms He's present!), believe in Him, and point others to Him, rather than looking to ourselves and getting swallowed up by our own circumstances.

In closing, spend time in prayer over YHWH's name and the perspective we have gained from "who am I?" versus "Who the I AM is."

Date of completion: _____

CHAPTER 4

If I believe the I AM *already* is _____, then I am _____.

Now Jesus did many other signs in the presence of the disciples, which are not written in this book; but these are written so that you may believe that Jesus is the Christ, the Son of God, and that by believing you may have life in his name. (John 20:30-31)

Afraid of the "deep end" of the water, but determined to make her daddy proud, the four-year old stood on the side of the pool, shivering. She shivered from the chill in the air, but more so from the fear that threatened to consume her. Warnings from her mom about not going near the pool without floaties or without mommy or daddy, echoed in her mind... Stories from her big brother about just how deep the deep end of the pool was, reminded her to be cautious.

Gone were the days of her fearless leaps into the kiddie pool. The near-drowning that one day left her nervous to even get into the bath water sometimes.

However, after repeated assurances from her daddy, she felt ready to jump. "Just look at me and jump to me. I will not let you fall. Don't look at the water. Don't think about anything else. You know me. You know I won't let anything happen to you. I love you, sweetheart. You can do this!"

A deep look into her father's eyes gave her a glimpse into his soul and the truthfulness of his words. She squeezed her eyes tight, bent her knees, and jumped.

Squeals of glee escaped from the little girl's lips as she splashed into her daddy's waiting arms. **Even with her eyes closed, she looked to her father, who never took his eyes from his daughter.**

> *"When we lift our inward eyes to gaze upon God we are sure to meet friendly eyes gazing back at us."*[2] **(A. W. Tozer)**

Is It Really Belief?

What if the little girl had responded, "I believe you, daddy, but I am not going to jump." Would that really be belief?

According to James 2:19, the demons can check all the boxes of belief. They even shudder.

What would happen if the demons looked *to* God instead of just looking *at* Him?

What does that kind of "belief" look like? (The rest of the verses in James 2:14-26 will inform your answer.)

---

[2] A. W. Tozer, *The Pursuit of God* (Chicago: Moody Publishers, 2015), 96.

The demons know *about* the I AM, but they don't *know* Him. Belief and faith stem from who the I AM is. And the more we know Him, the more we believe in Him. The I AM reveals Himself throughout the Bible through His eternal characteristics, and later through the incarnation—all with the goal of relationship.

How was the little girl able to believe her daddy?

Looking and Believing

A powerful story in the book of Numbers speaks to the concept of looking and believing. Read Numbers 21:4-9.

What were the Israelites focused on (Num. 21:4-5)? In other words, what were they *not* looking to?

When Jesus is speaking to Nicodemus, He compares Himself to the bronze snake. What is the correlation between the bronze snake and Jesus (Num. 21:9b; John 3:14-15)?

Using these same verses, what did the Israelites do that we are now called to do?

As A.W. Tozer points out in the chapter "The Gaze of the Soul," in his book, *The Pursuit of God,*

...look and believe are synonymous terms. "Looking" on the Old Testament serpent is identical with "believing" on the New Testament Christ. That is, the looking and the believing are the same thing... while Israel looked with their external eyes, believing is done with the heart... faith is the gaze of a soul upon a saving God.[3]

What parallels do you see between the concepts of looking and believing?

Belief is about the I AM we look to, not the "eye" (or I) that does the looking. In contrast, unbelief puts self where God should be.

> *We can look where we're stepping, or*
> *we can look to the One who guides our steps.*
>
> *We can focus on where we think we're going,*
> *or we can focus on the One who leads our lives.*
>
> *We can be distracted by doubt, or we can be directed by Truth.*
>
> *We can see the problem, or we can look to the Problem-Solver.*

From the Common Threads: What is a name or characteristic of the I AM that you will **grow and bloom** in your belief of?

---

3 A. W. Tozer, *The Pursuit of God* (Chicago: Moody Publishers, 2015), 93.

Belief isn't about Seeing, but Looking

When the servant of the man of God got up and went out early the next morning, an army with horses and chariots had surrounded the city. "Oh no, my lord! What shall we do?" the servant asked.

"Don't be afraid," the prophet answered. "Those who are with us are more than those who are with them."

And Elisha prayed, "Open his eyes, LORD, so that he may see." Then the LORD opened the servant's eyes, and he looked and saw the hills full of horses and chariots of fire all around Elisha. (2 Kings 6:15-17)

We don't know if Elisha could see with his physical eyes that the army of the Lord surrounded them. But we do know that he looked with eyes of faith.

Having trouble seeing with eyes of faith? We can echo the prayer of the father in Mark 9:23-24.

"If you can'?" said Jesus. "Everything is possible for one who believes."

Immediately the boy's father exclaimed, "I do believe; help me overcome my unbelief!"

Belief can be defined as looking beyond what we can see. How does 2 Corinthians 5:7 phrase that concept?

Faith is seeing the Unseen and believing in Him. Hebrews 11:1 affirms this definition and then enumerates those whose testimonies of belief profess that faith. Yet it is easy to lose eyes of faith when we focus on what our physical eyes see.

Walk by faith, not by sight, literally

After returning from a trip to Buenos Aires, Argentina, and Bogotá, Colombia, my vision was so blurred that I became afraid that I was losing my sight completely. I wrestled with what this apparent blindness implied for my physical body and my ability to work.

Desperate for answers, I visited a second-generation optometrist, who was equally baffled until he discovered a rare virus on my corneas. Grateful to have "unveiled" the reason for my blurred vision, my grappling continued: My vision and my prognosis were still unclear.

Finally, as the blurriness began to subside, eye fatigue and eye strain continued to be factors, and seeing detail, especially to read, was nearly impossible.

Much of what I do in life and in ministry is dependent on eyesight. No matter how good a typist I claim to be, I need to be able to proof what I have written—whether for a blog post, a thank-you note, or the lessons I am working on.

There is much value in the Word that is written in my heart, but I was still unable to read and study the Word as I would like, whether for a devotional thought or in preparation for the next book.

I wrestled with feelings of guilt and frustration—mostly because, yet again, I was focused on a dependence on my own abilities. I was quite literally reminded that I must walk by faith, not by sight.

In what ways are you depending on your own abilities—your "sight"—instead of walking by faith?

From the Common Threads: What **thorn** is blinding your eyes of faith?

Eyes of Faith

Read the story of the man born blind in John 9.

According to the disciples, how did they see the man born blind (John 9:1-2)?

How did Jesus see the man born blind (John 9:3-5)?

How did the man born blind see Jesus (John 9:6-12)?

How did the Pharisees see Jesus (John 9:13-16)? What lens or filter were they looking through?

How did the parents of the man born blind see the situation (John 9:18-23)?

How did Jesus see the Pharisees (John 9:39-41)?

Which Eyes are You Using?

The blind man sought out Jesus later to express his belief and worship Him (John 9:35-38). By his obedience, washing in the Pool of Siloam, the blind man looked with eyes of faith. The Pharisees looked at Jesus, but their perspective was warped because they looked through the distorted filter of their own interpretation of Scripture.

Using eyes of belief, like those of the man born blind, describe a time when your circumstances could've been interpreted differently if not looked at with eyes of faith. Make note of how the story is told through the eyes of faith (looking in belief to the I AM) vs. the story told *without* looking to the I AM. Note: This is another testimony of belief!

Blinded by Fear or Looking to the I AM

It is easy to get confused or distracted. We think we are seeing things clearly, but unless we look to and believe in the I AM, we misinterpret things.

When we are weary, for example, our sight fails us. We lose perspective.

> *Fear, discouragement, and overwhelming feelings cloud our judgement and cause us to forget who the I AM already is.*

Consumed by fear, a sister in failing health explained the burden of being "the spiritual thread that holds her family together..." Fear had paralyzed her from doing anything; but on New Year's Eve, she called the local church and asked for prayers: the first step toward conquering the state of fear she lived in. Taking one step at a time, she is no longer alone in her struggle to look to God who is greater than all her fears.

From the Common Threads: Sometimes it can be hard to ask for help. What are ways in which an Iron Rose Sister can serve as **iron sharpening iron** and encourage you to **dig deeper** in your relationship with the I AM?

Courage is not the absence of fear; rather it is the bravery to step forward in spite of fears.

"Aunt M, I Scared"

My nephew was playing on the floor with his cars while I was eating my dinner. A storm was brewing and the wind was blowing. There was thunder, but no lightning or rain yet. Thunderstorms are not as common in Denver, Colorado, where we lived at the time, as they are in Louisiana, where I grew up. So, I began to explain thunder, lightning, and storms in a way that a two-and-a-half-year-old could understand.

Kadesh was graciously listening with an occasional acknowledgement of my words, but he was mostly paying attention to his cars—until a train came by at the same time as a peal of thunder roared.

"Aunt M, I scared." Kadesh gathered his cars and trotted across the kitchen to come sit in my lap.

"Why are you scared?"

"The train."

"You like trains. Why did the train scare you?"

"I scared," was all he would repeat as he snuggled in my arms.

For me, it didn't matter what had scared him or why he was scared. I wasn't going to reprimand him for being scared. He knew where he could go to be comforted and I delighted in his snuggles and trust in me.

It brought about a moment of clarity for me... Sometimes I beat myself up for being scared. But God doesn't reprimand me for my fear—instead, He longs for me to go to Him with my fears in order to be truly comforted. He relishes the moments when we come to Him, curl up in his lap, and rest our heads on his chest, trusting in the One who can protect us from whatever we are afraid of.

Take a moment today to bring to YHWH whatever you are fearful of. He will not reprimand you for your fears, but rather rejoice in the fact that you allowed your trust in Him to be greater than your fear.

We can find ourselves afraid of fear. **However, fear provides us the opportunity to overcome our fears by going to the One who is greater than all our fears!**

When we trust in God, His perfect love drives out fear (1 John 4:18). We look to Him instead of looking at whatever causes the fear.

What fear-filled situation are you facing?

What facet of God's character speaks to those fears?

What happens when we look to the I AM instead of focusing on the fears?

Fill in the blank below:

If I believe the I AM *already* is _____,
then I have nothing to fear.

A Change in Perspective/Seeing through the I AM's Lens

When I look to the I AM and believe...

➤ My voice of complaint is transformed into a spirit of gratitude for YHWH Provider.

➤ The weight of life's issues is an opportunity to give that weight over to YHWH Comforter, Father, and Friend.

➤ The stress of any situation is a prompt to leave YHWH Almighty in control and recognize that my frustration stems from my meager attempts to take the reins of His perfect design.

➤ The speed of the spinning carousel is a reminder that YHWH Lord of Hosts can handle more than one spinning plate at a time.

Write out your own version of one of the above sentences (or make your own!) transforming a current circumstance into a testimony of belief in the I AM.

Can we believe what we don't know? Yes, because that is the definition of faith. Nevertheless, it is easier to believe when I do know the One in whom I believe. Belief is about looking to the Unseen because it is what is truly real, versus getting lost in what we see with our physical eyes (2 Cor. 4:18).

And John gives us that invitation—to get to know the I AM and by believing in Him, have life in His name (John 20:30-31). **The entire**

focus of the book of John is centered around who the I AM is and the testimonies of those who believed in the I AM incarnate.

Summarizing some of Chuck Swindoll's insights from the book of John,

> "The Greek word pisteuō, translated "believe," appears 98 times in the Gospel of John—multiple times per chapter... The term pisteuō means "to acknowledge the truth as truth." It also, more importantly, means "to trust, to rely upon, to derive confidence in" something or someone. When I say I believe in Jesus Christ, I declare that I trust Him, I rely upon Him, I have placed my complete confidence in Him; everything I know about this life and whatever occurs after death is dependent upon His claims about Himself and how I respond to His offer of grace."[4]

I Believe, Help Me Overcome My Unbelief (Mark 9:24)

Let's go back to John chapter 1. Make a list of the names or characteristics we see in the 1st chapter of John for God, YHWH, or the I AM incarnate (Jesus). (I found 12!)

Pick two of these names or qualities of God from John 1 and describe what this implies for your own identity and purpose. What questions are answered from those descriptions and explanations? Feel free to use the following format or put things in your own words. You can also draw it or illustrate these concepts in a creative way.

4 Charles R. Swindoll, "Insights on John," *Swindoll Living Insights New Testament Commentary*, Volume 4 (Carol Stream, Illinois: Tyndale House Publishers, 2014), 9-10.

If I believe the I AM *already* is _____, then I am _____.

Growing belief comes from the continued practice of looking to the I AM, seeing with His eyes, and looking through His lens to view everything else from His perspective.

I look to You, help me overcome the distractions.

I seek You, help me overcome my selfish focus.

I trust You, help me overcome my fears.

I believe You, help me overcome my unbelief.

Date of completion: _____

CHAPTER 5

How Can You Ask Me for a Drink? The Living Water

The woman said to him, "I know that Messiah is coming (he who is called Christ). When he comes, he will tell us all things." Jesus said to her, "I who speak to you am he." (John 4:25-26)

Who Do You Think You Are?

Several dignitaries attended a large formal gala. The party attendees exceeded the kitchen's expected number of guests, but the kitchen was stocked well, save for a thin amount of butter. The Head Chef instructed the waiters to give each guest only one pat of butter, even if they asked for more. And given that some wouldn't take butter they should have "just enough."

A waiter began serving and came upon an older man and his wife. The wife asked if she could have more butter. The waiter began replying politely:

"I'm sorry ma'am, we are running a little low tonight due to the unexpected attendance and..."

Upon hearing his wife's request refused, her husband, cutting the waiter off mid-sentence, stood up and got in the waiter's face.

"EXCUSE ME, DO YOU KNOW WHO I AM?" asked the old man in a condescending tone.

The dumbfounded waiter recoiled and earnestly said, "Well, no sir I don't."

The old man became larger, straightened his shoulders, and wagged his finger near the waiter's face as he expounded:

"I'm Senator Smith from the greatest state in the union. I am the head of this committee, and the chair of that committee. My family has been running our state for decades. I authorized the funding for this very gala. I've met with leaders of foreign states. I've negotiated diplomatic treaties and I don't expect my wife to be talked down to by some ...err waiter who is getting uppity."

Listening to this tirade the waiter patiently summoned up his courage and rather than buckle under the intimidation, kindly said,

"Thank you, Senator Smith, but perhaps you do not know who I am."

The Senator growled back and with a tone of derision asked, **"Who is it you think you are?"**

"I'm the man with the butter," replied the waiter, leaving the Senator stunned as he quietly walked off to continue waiting tables.

Clash of the Classes

The encounter between the senator and the waiter stands in stark contrast to the conversation between Jesus and the woman at the well in John 4. However, the disparity of position and status does carry some parallels.

Read John 4:1-30 and make a list of what we know about Jesus and the Samaritan woman. Think about their descriptions and list the ways in which they are opposite in their respective circles below (on each side). Then find some things they have in common, like they're both thirsty, and list them in the overlapping middle area.

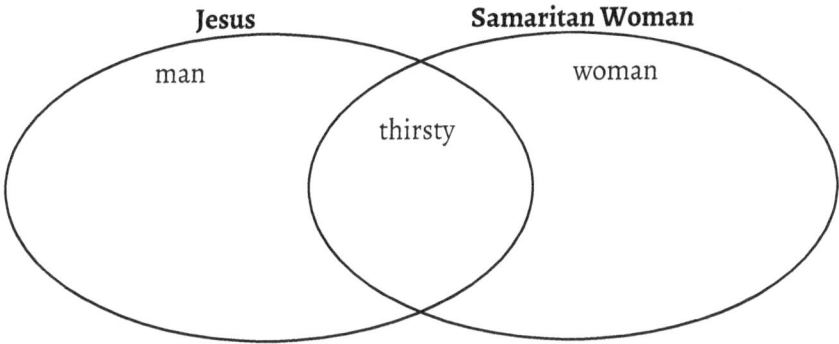

Jesus   **Samaritan Woman**

man   woman

thirsty

Mixed Motivation

Now, look back through John 4:1-30 and we are going to make some observations about their conversation.

There are multiple interpretations of the woman's motivation and reactions. Check which of the following you think describes her demeanor or her attitude, as displayed through her questions and answers. Feel free to select more than one and cross out any you think do not describe her.

___ Avoiding/Deflecting   ___ Knowledgeable

___ Bold   ___ Perceptive

___ Confused   ___ Respectful

___ Curious   ___ Sarcastic

___ Defensive   ___ Sincere

___ Fearful   ___ Uneducated

___ Focused on the physical   ___ Other: _____

Through the text, we get some insights into the Samaritan woman's current life circumstance, but spend a moment reflecting on what her past might've been like, the story behind the story. Are there any other words you would use to describe the woman and her conversation with Jesus?

No matter how we have described the Samaritan woman, Jesus definitely saw her through a different lens than the rest of the townspeople she was avoiding at that noon hour. Christ's perspective was spiritual; His focus was clear. By looking always to His Father, the I AM Living Water saw the woman for who she was: thirsty, yes, but also a valuable instrument in God's kingdom.

> *Jesus used "the outcast" for outreach.*

Therefore, Jesus' motivation was clear: "He had to pass through Samaria" (John 4:4). She wanted to hide, but she could never escape from YHWH's presence and attention.

What do the following two passages say about the I AM?

Jeremiah 23:23-24

Psalm 139:7-10

Have you ever felt like you were the outcast?

Jesus honored a seeker who didn't know what questions to ask.

What characteristics of Jesus speak to the questions the Samaritan woman asked—or even the questions she didn't verbalize, but Jesus knew she was asking?

Jesus offered Himself as Living Water—not the stagnant water in the well, but water that brings life. The Presence of YHWH was made known as the fulfillment of one of our most basic needs—water.

WATER...

For this next section, I would like to recommend you go get a glass of water to have with you while you read and study. We will pause for a moment occasionally to take a drink and reflect, but don't drink any yet. Yes, I'm serious. I'll wait. Don't get distracted by the laundry while you go get your water. Just get it and come right back. And don't take a drink—tempting as it may be.

Water, Water, Everywhere and Not a Drop to Drink

Welcome back! Thanks for humoring me by getting a glass of water. For this next section, please leave your water there, untouched.

A riddle is shared with elementary students, "Water, water everywhere and not a drop to drink. Where am I?"

The answer is the ocean. Marooned on a raft, an individual can die of thirst surrounded by the salty sea water. Have you ever been to the beach and after swimming in the ocean, your lips feel cracked, and even though you are wet, your mouth feels dry? When you finally come in for a drink or a snack, you drink deeply of your refreshing cool drink and then are refreshed to go back out again?

Don't drink your water yet. Take a moment and stay on the sun-scorched beach. Or imagine yourself on a hot, humid day at summer camp, drenched in sweat from sports. Maybe you are in another country on a 100-degree day with no air conditioning, sitting under a metal roof, vacillating between turning the fan off and on because "on" means it is blowing hot air, but "off" means there is no air moving. Yep. Been there. Done that. Miserable.

Don't drink your water yet! Reflect on the thirst you are feeling right now and the time you have felt most thirsty in your life.

Write down how it feels to be that thirsty. Have you ever reached a point where you were beyond thirst?

Now, go ahead and take a slow drink of water. Savor it. Contemplate it.

How did that feel? What thoughts come to mind as you drink the water? Jot some of those thoughts down.

Physical Water/Living Water

At the top of my "things I am thankful for" list, you will always find water. I drink a lot of water and I am blessed to have access to clean water. I love being able to take a hot shower and others appreciate my attitude when I haven't had to endure a cold one...

unless it is a scorching hot day in Central America and then bring on the cold water!

Because of the times when I have had limited access to water or had to work diligently to ensure that it was safe or clean, I appreciate it all the more.

Our bodies need water; we crave water. Without water, our physical bodies cannot function properly.

Even though I am what we jokingly call a "good kind of heavy drinker," I can get distracted in what I am working on and forget to stop and take a drink. "I'll finish this one more thing, then I'll go get a drink."

Some time later, my thirst neglected, I feel parched and dry, even weak or hungry, all because I have not drunk enough water. At that point, I begin to crave different foods and try to satisfy my thirst with a cup of tea or a snack, but what I really need is a big glass of water.

When I am not partaking of the Living Water on a consistent basis, I feel spiritually parched and dry, weak or hungry. And unfortunately, I often neglect to turn to the source of Living Water that is always present right there, waiting for me. The I AM Living Water, who was and is and is to come, quenches the thirst I may or may not know I have.

Without the Living Water, we suffer from spiritual dehydration.

The Danger of Dehydration

As a general rule, I know a lot of complainers. I must confess that I fall into that trap myself on occasion. When the Israelites begged for water, God heard their cries and directed Moses to strike the rock in order to draw water from it. Turn to Exodus 17:1-7 and read this story for yourself.

Where does the Exodus 17 story fall in the sequence of the history of the Israelites? (Where have they been and where are they going?)

Which name of God is used here? (Don't forget to pay attention to any capital letters.)

Where exactly does God say that the water will come from—where is the rock?

Where else do we see that place mentioned? (Hint: Exodus 3:1, 12)

In Exodus 3:12, what does YHWH say will happen on that mountain?

But, as we see in Exodus 17:1-7, what did the Israelites actually do on that mountain?

What else later happens on this same mountain, also known as Mt. Sinai (Ex. 20; Ex. 32)?

What comes to mind as you reflect on YHWH's revelations in this location, especially as they contrast with Moses' and the Israelites' actions?

Living Water Forever

Remember, the I AM, YHWH, Yahweh, LORD, the One who rescued His people from oppression in Egypt, is the Living Water. He is the One who transcends all time, space, or other limitations. The I AM Living Water is, was, and always will be.

Using the following verses that describe Living Water from the Old Testament (was), New Testament (is) and Revelation (will be), what do we learn about YHWH?

Jeremiah 17:13

John 4:10; John 7:37

Revelation 7:17; 22:6, 17

Sharing the Living Water

Considering the blessing and efficacy of Living Water, how can we selfishly keep it to ourselves? We each know someone who is thirsty. And if I truly believe that the I AM Living Water satisfies that thirst, I am motivated and inspired to share it with others.

When I believe in His name—knowing, trusting and acting on that belief—I share it (James 2:14-26).

We also believe in hydrogen and oxygen, which make water, but it is not something we consciously think about or "believe in" such that it would impact our lives. However, the I AM Creator puts oxygen and hydrogen together in a way that allows us to be physically *and* spiritually nourished. Truly believing in the I AM Living Water impacts us!

How does (or should) knowing and believing in the I AM Living Water impact our daily lives?

Her Testimony of Belief

As we conclude this chapter, turn back with me to John 4 and read verses 28-30 and 39-42.

What was the testimony of the woman at the well?

What did the Samaritan woman do with her testimony?

How did others respond to her testimony initially (John 4:30)?

What became the testimony of belief for the members of the town (John 4:42)?

From Outcast to Outreach

The Samaritan woman demonstrates how the I AM calls the outcast, the unlikely, and the unequipped to do His work.

Read the following verses and write out 1) who the I AM called and 2) how that person verbally responded. If you are familiar with their story, reflect on what made each of them an outcast, as well.

Genesis 22:1, 11

Exodus 3:4

1 Samuel 3:4-10

Isaiah 6:8

How does the I AM ask us to respond to His call? Remember: He specializes in using the outcasts for outreach!

Through your own testimony of belief in the I AM, name three ways and three individuals with whom you can share your belief in the I AM this next week.

Common Threads

As we get to know and believe the I AM more deeply each week, we also have the opportunity to connect with one another. For the Common Threads this week, we are leaving them together. We want to focus on the application of being iron sharpening iron as we encourage one another to share Living Water with someone else. You can do like Jesus and invite the person to share in a physical drink (coffee, tea, or a simple glass of water) in order to speak about the source of Living Water: the I AM. And you can practice sharing your testimony of belief with your Iron Rose Sisters by explaining what the Living Water means to you.

A name or characteristic of the I AM that you will **grow and bloom** in your belief of:

Removing the **thorn** of a flawed perspective or distracted focus:

Ways in which an Iron Rose Sister can serve as **iron sharpening iron** and encourage you to **dig deeper** in your relationship with the I AM:

A verse, word of encouragement, or reminder of the I AM:

Date of completion: _____

CHAPTER 6

Will My Needs Be Met?
The Bread of Life

Jesus said to them, "I am the bread of life; whoever comes to me shall not
hunger, and whoever believes in me shall never thirst. (John 6:35)

Your Shoes Will Not Wear Out

A peaceful state in God's right hand comes when we trust His provision. The I AM gave my family a concrete example of that when I was in high school...

Dad had lost his job in corporate downsizing after having worked for the same company for fourteen years. We were all in shock and his job search lasted a year and a half.

In the meantime, mom recertified and took a job at as a special education teacher in an inner-city elementary school; we girls rotated cooking dinner and other household responsibilities; and we all got creative in our spending—or lack thereof.

Through it all, the I AM's provision was astounding and humbling...

During the stressful, yet joyful year and a half, each and every one of our needs were met without fail—sometimes anonymously and at other times through our Christian brothers and sisters.

Always on her feet as a teacher, my mom valued her comfortable shoes for standing and worked to make them last. One afternoon after school, she took her worn pair of shoes to the cobbler wanting to stretch their usefulness as long as possible.

"Well, ma'am. I can stitch them here, but they'll come apart over there. I can glue this, but it's not going to hold. There's really nothing more I can do with these shoes. I think it's time to get a new pair."

Mom returned to the van where we girls were waiting, "Ladies, our forty years in the wilderness are about up. God promised the Israelites that their shoes would not wear out (Deut. 29:5). My shoes have finally worn out, so it must be time for your dad to get a job."

One month later, he did.

As soon as my dad got a job, each of my sisters hit a growth spurt (aged 14, 12, and 6 at the time), I left for college, and mom got a new pair of shoes for teaching.

> *YHWH Jireh means the LORD Provides. And the I AM's provision is always perfect—in His way, in His timing.*

Provision in YHWH's Right Hand

I have been fascinated with God's right hand for years now. Actually, one of the other Iron Rose Sister Ministries Bible study books is entitled, *In God's Right Hand: Whom Shall I Fear?* in which I explore the more than sixty times across the Old and New Testaments we see a reference to God's right hand.

One such instance of a reference to God's right hand illustrates our insight into the I AM this week. Turn with me to Exodus 15. As you read verses 1-21, make note of the following:

1. At least three names of God mentioned (pay special attention to whether the name is listed in CAPS or not):

2. What the LORD's right hand did:

3. At least three descriptions of the I AM, as revealed through His deeds:

Now, what one word would you use to describe Exodus 15:1-21?

Not Only Israel's Vicious Cycle

Deliverance, Celebration, Victorious, Glorious, Powerful, Awesome... I am sure you came up with many excellent words to describe the scene and song with the Israelites in Exodus 15:1-21—all in honor of who the I AM was, is, and will be.

Famous author, speaker, and Bible student, Chuck Swindoll used the word "Abundance" to summarize Exodus 15:1-21.[5] It is what he and other scholars describe as the first stage of the cycle in which we often find the Israelites and ourselves.

Time and time again, consistently across the Old Testament, we see the Israelites cycle through five stages. Thankfully, these stages can be found summarized in one single chapter: Exodus 15. The brevity of the Exodus chapter and its proximity to one of our primary stories highlighting the I AM, the Bread of Life, this week make it a great starting place for the focus of this section.

Let's define the five stages in the cycle and see how they relate to the I AM's provision as the Bread of Life. Read the rest of Exodus 15, verses 22-27, and observe the Israelites and their conversations with Moses.

Stage 1, Exodus 15:1-21   Abundance/Deliverance/Celebration

Stage 2, Exodus 15:22   Expectation

Stage 3, Exodus 15:23   Disappointment

Stage 4, Exodus 15:24   Complaint

Stage 5, Exodus 15:25-27   Provision

Do you agree with these descriptions of the five stages? Why or why not? Is there a better word you would choose for any of them?

5 Charles R. Swindoll, *The Swindoll Study Bible* (Carol Stream, Illinois: Tyndale House Publishers, 2017).

Our wilderness may look different depending on our stage of life or struggle of the day, but I believe we are each somewhere in this cycle at any given moment.

How have you seen the stages of this cycle play out in your life? What stage are you in right now?

Escaping Egypt

When facing a time of expectation, I can slip into an attitude of entitlement. My disappointment quickly becomes frustration—not just at God, but with myself. And when I reach the stage of complaint, I often turn my complaints on others instead of turning to YHWH, looking to Him and believing in the I AM.

He who was and is and is to come has ALWAYS provided in the past. Remember? "I *already* AM." So why do I consistently fall back into the trap of doubt and cycle through the other stages? Ladies, we are escaping Egypt together—not just a time of persecution, but also any bad habits we picked up during that time.

YHWH invites us to break destructive cycles and believe in Him completely. And He provides us with the steps to do so.

What is the condition of the promise in Exodus 15:26?

How does the LORD identify Himself in Exodus 15:26, before He leads His people to provision?

What does healing have to do with provision?

> *When we are blinded by our needs and wants, we cannot see our brokenness in need of healing, our weakness in need of strength, nor our deficiencies in need of YHWH Jireh's provision.*

We allow our expectations, disappointments, and complaints to overshadow the I AM's abundant provision.

And when we grumble and complain, we have lost our perspective...

Count Your Blessings or Complain, Complain, Again

Exodus 16 takes place one month after leaving Egypt. And while they are physically located in the wilderness of Sin and less than exemplary in their behavior, it is worth clarifying that "Sin" is a geographical reference to the Sinai region and not to a sinful state of being.

Make a list of five things you are grateful for.

Now write down two things that are current stresses in your life.

Read back over your grateful list. Does it feel overshadowed by your stresses? Where is our focus? Do we see the blessings and provision clearly?

Looking back at what we are grateful for or counting our blessings is a powerful exercise. However, 20/20 hindsight only works when you are thinking clearly. Do you listen well or think clearly when you are hungry?

I have a friend who used to call it my Dr. Jekyll/Mr. Hyde syndrome. This was before the term "hangry" became popular. When my blood sugar would get low, either my patience wore thin and my answers were shorter, or I would be dragging and unable to carry on an intelligent conversation. My friend would graciously help me find a snack before things got worse.

I had to be careful to not allow that explanation to become an excuse to fall into bad habits, negative attitudes, and destructive thinking. I had the choice to count my blessings or complain, complain, again, blinded by my hunger.

From the Common Threads: What **thorn** of a bad habit or destructive thought process needs to be removed?

You may have read Exodus 16 in a children's Bible school class, either as a child or in teaching this lesson to the children. However, there are many adult-level applications from this story. Read all of

Exodus 16—a powerful narrative of YHWH Jireh's patience and provision.

The Israelites are hungry in Exodus 16:3, but what evidence do we see of them not thinking clearly or using selective memory?

One take-away from this chapter is the admonition to *"Look forward in faith—not backward with selective amnesia."*[6]

What other lessons do we learn from the Israelites or what characteristics of the I AM are revealed in Exodus 16?

From the Common Threads: What characteristic of the I AM do you want to **grow and bloom** in your belief of?

Describe the manna—not just physically, but what the name meant and what it represented.

---

[6] Charles R. Swindoll, *The Swindoll Study Bible* (Carol Stream, Illinois: Tyndale House Publishers, 2017).

What is It? Bread?

The Israelites ate manna in the desert. And God also provided quail. He meets our needs and goes beyond the most basic level of provision.

Yet the manna and the quail were incomplete. They were a mere foreshadowing of the Bread of Life—the I AM incarnate—who became flesh and dwelt among us. Turn with me to John 6 as we spend the rest of our time at the feet of Jesus, revealing Himself and inviting us to truly believe in Him, the Bread of Life.

Yet another story popular in children's classes, read John 6:1-14, focusing on the concept of belief.

How do each of the following characters in the story show their belief, and at what point do they believe (or not)? Remember: Jesus often tests in order to teach.

Jesus

Disciples

The people/crowd

Looking at the next section of John 6, verses 15-26, what do each of those same characters do with their belief? Does the belief continue or waver? Did it reveal what they really believed in to begin with?

(Continued space on next page)

What is the I AM's teaching in John 6:27-34? What does He say is of utmost importance?

How does the I AM compare to the manna from Exodus 16?

Read John 6:47-51. What does it mean for you that Jesus, the I AM, YHWH incarnate, is the Bread of Life? Think about the correlation between bread and life. Reflect on the impact this belief has in your daily life.

The Manna Who *Was*, the Bread of Life Who *Is*, and the Life that *Is to Come*

Eternal life is not just about heaven. Life and eternal life are used interchangeably throughout the Book of John. We don't have to be about the "waiting" for eternal life. We now have access to "true bread from heaven" as Jesus Himself stated in John 6:32-33. This bread gives life.

In many parts of the world, it is easy to comprehend the terminology that Jesus is the bread of life. However, for a southerner in the U.S., Jesus may be the biscuit or the cornbread of life.

When I am traveling in Latin America or speaking to women in the Latina culture, I love to present a new twist on John 6:35. I propose that in Mexico, Jesus is the *tortilla* of life; in El Salvador, Jesus is the *pupusa* of life. And, my favorite: In Venezuela, Jesus is the *arepa* of life!

If you don't know what those foods are, I invite you to meet someone who can share the deliciousness of each one! Each is a staple, foundational to the local diet. As with breads in different regions, some are made with corn, flour, or other grains. They are combined with other ingredients to make culinary delights that tickle our taste buds.

What does it mean that I AM, the Bread of Life, is daily life and eternal life?

Jesus affirms that we need daily nourishment—physically and spiritually—in order to live an abundant life.

Our Daily Bread

"Give us this day, our daily bread," from the Lord's Prayer (Matt. 6:11), is a request that God provide for our physical and our spiritual needs.

List three examples of how to partake of the Bread of Life on a daily basis.

What would happen if you only ate one day a week?

Every first day of the week, we gather to eat of the bread and drink the cup in remembrance of the True Bread of Life. When we gather for the Lord's Supper, we are reminded to look to Him, to believe in Him, and to have life in His name.

> *YHWH Bread of Life invites us into relationship and into belief in His name through His death, burial, and resurrection.*

Yet our belief cannot be relegated to a mere hour on Sundays in which we remember the One in whom we believe. **The I AM, YHWH, LORD, Bread of Life is the daily provision of spiritual nourishment and the source of life.**

From the Common Threads: What are ways in which an Iron Rose Sister can serve as **iron sharpening iron** and encourage you to **dig deeper** in your relationship with the I AM, the Bread of Life?

Provision for Refugees

I will close with one more story of God's provision. I mentioned how Venezuelans eat and value *arepas*, their "bread," which is made out of a finely ground precooked cornmeal. Unfortunately, at the time of publication of this book, in that country, it is nearly impossible to obtain the primary ingredient necessary to make them.

People across the world have become familiar with *arepas* as they get to know Venezuelans who have fled their home country in escape of the humanitarian crisis triggered by a political and economic crisis. These Venezuelan refugees are striving to make the best of their new lives as they have left everything, including family and friends, in search of a better future.

The refugee crisis is unprecedented in many parts of the world. The people of various countries are suffering and while God can be glorified through it all, it can be challenging to keep our eyes fixed on YHWH Jireh, our Provider and the Bread of Life.

One refugee family fled to a neighboring country because of the lack of resources in their homeland. The husband, wife, and their two young sons made a life for themselves in their new residence, adopting some of the local customs, while still maintaining their faith in God.

In time, the two young men married local women and shared their faith with them. They praised the God of their fathers for His blessing.

A short time later, tragedy struck and both young men were killed. The father also died leaving three widows, each shattered by tremendous suffering and loss. Embittered by her deep anguish, the mother decided to return to her home country.

The young widows planned to accompany their mother-in-law, but she begged them to return to their families. One daughter-in-law was unwavering in her resolve.

"Do not urge me to leave you or to return from following you. For where you go I will go, and where you lodge I will lodge. Your people shall be my people, and your God my God. Where you die I will die, and there will I be buried. May the LORD *do so to me and more also if anything but death parts me from you."* (Ruth 1:16-17)

The next three chapters of Ruth tell the story of the I AM's provision, hope, and eternal plan (promises of the I AM that continue today). As the story of Ruth concludes, we recognize that Boaz, Ruth's second husband and kinsman-redeemer, is a foreshadowing of Christ, our Redeemer and Provider.

At different points in the story, Naomi and Ruth each doubted God's provision. Yet their testimony of belief became part of the genealogy and ancestry of Christ![7]

What is your testimony of belief this week? When have you seen YHWH Jireh's provision in your life? (Don't forget there is additional space in the Notes/Testimonies section at the back of this book.)

As we grow and bloom in our belief in the I AM's provision, may we encourage each other, just as Ruth and Naomi did, with our testimonies of belief. They were an early example of Iron Rose

---

7 An in-depth study of Ruth and Naomi and their relationship is available for free download as an e-Petal study "Iron Rose Sisters: A Deeper Look at Ruth and Naomi" on Iron Rose Sister Ministries' website: www.IronRoseSister.com

Sisters, taking turns being the strong one, but ultimately pointing each other to focus on the I AM. May we, too, serve as iron sharpening iron, inspiring one another to be as beautiful as roses in God's abundant garden, in spite of the thorns.

Date of completion: _____

CHAPTER 7

Am I Seeing Clearly?
The Light of the World

Again Jesus spoke to them, saying, "I am the light of the world. Whoever follows me will not walk in darkness, but will have the light of life."
(John 8:12)

A sunflower turns its face to the sun during every stage of its growth. It grows tall to reach for the sun. Its stem is strong, yet flexible, able to rotate at the top so that the bloomed flower can swivel with the sun and then bow to rest when the sun has set.

In Spanish, the word for sunflower—*girasol*—literally translates "turns to the sun," reflecting its identity and purpose. The sunflower is drawn to the light, craves the light, and follows the light. Unable to live without the light, the sunflower has no other thought than to go toward the source of light, the sun, which also provides nourishment for its growth.

Just as the sunflower needs the light to survive, turning toward its warming rays, the Light of Life offers an invitation to participate in the abundant life the I AM offers. When we look to the true source of light, we grow and maintain our focus. Everything else is put in perspective—we see clearly, maybe for the first time.

Do we look to and believe in the I AM, the Light of the World, to the degree a sunflower does? Why or why not? When or when not?

Write out our key verse for this lesson: John 8:12. (Feel free to choose a different version than the one quoted at the beginning of this chapter, ESV.)

A stranger to a new city, the college graduate explores downtown choosing to walk down the well-lit streets instead of the dimly lit ones. Why? What is it about the light we are drawn to?

What happens when someone is not drawn to the light? What happens in the darkness?

Light and Dark

What was the first thing that the I AM created? (See Gen. 1:1-5.)

What else do we learn about the I AM and Light in the beginning from John 1:1-13?

Light and dark, good and evil, clarity and confusion, enlightenment and ignorance... What else comes to mind when we think about light and darkness?

What is the power of light?

Purposes of the Light

Did you know that one cannot actually "see" light? Rather light allows us to see everything else because of how light reflects off of the object. Photographers, painters, and other artists pay special attention to this truth as they carefully craft their interpretations of reality, toying with the way light dances off of and highlights the facets of their creations. Even the colors we see and perceive are a reflection and refraction of light.

While visiting the eye doctor, he assessed whether I needed readers. Not emotionally ready to face that stage of life, I was relieved when he turned on a small light near the text that he asked me to read. While it was unclear and slightly fuzzy in the dim lighting, the additional light allowed me to read the words clearly. I breathed a sigh of relief when he pronounced, "It looks like you are compensating adequately at this point. We'll check again next time, but for now, you don't need readers. A little extra light is all you need."

Physical light can give us a clearer picture of what we are looking at. Spiritual light clarifies things in an even more powerful way. The following verses expound upon spiritual truths revealed by physical light.

What does the refraction of light in Genesis 9:8-17 remind us of?

What was the purpose of the light in Exodus 13:21-22? And what form(s) did that light take?

What does the psalmist David compare to light and what is its purpose in Psalm 119:105?

What (and who) was revealed by the light in Acts 22:3-11 and to whom was it revealed?

Have you experienced a moment in which a physical light or the light of God's Word revealed something to you or helped you see more clearly? **Whether a promise, guidance, a call to repentance, or other revelation, it becomes a part of your testimony of belief!**

What has the Light of Life and of the World revealed in your life?

A Blinding Light

My eyes are quite sensitive. I wear polarized sunglasses in the rain in order to avoid the glare. I have a setting on my phone that allows me to dim the screen, especially useful at night in my dark room. On the rare occasion I look at something bright in the dark, the light sends a piercing pain through my eyes to the back of my head. The residual reflection of the light, like the flash from a camera, is visible for many more minutes, whether my eyes are open or closed.

The effects of light for someone who has grown accustomed to the darkness are drastic and painful. Our eyes cannot physically adjust that quickly to all that is exposed by the light. Our reaction is instantaneous and instinctual. We draw away from what is foreign and painful.

First thing in the morning, the bright light of a room may be a harsh greeting to a new day, but our eyes adjust, and we move forward seeing more clearly and able to navigate the room and our day.

> *For those who are walking in darkness, spiritually speaking, a negative reaction is to be expected.*

After getting past the initial shock of the revelation, illuminated by the light, one must decide what to do about it: embrace the light or reject it.

We see through various stories of healing in the New Testament that the demons avoided such exposure and begged Jesus to leave them alone (e.g. Mark 5:1-20). They longed for the darkness, but the I AM did not let them retain control over those He healed (e.g. Mark 9:14-29). **In contrast, those who welcomed the Light were transformed and healed.**

Transformed by Light

One such woman, Mary Magdalene, who was healed from seven demons (Mark 16:9; Luke 8:2), after experiencing the Light, believed and followed the Light—all the way to the cross, even after His disciples had abandoned Him (John 19:25).

Continuing John's account of this I AM follower, turn to John 20:1-18. Read this account paying special attention to Mary Magdalene's perspective—a seeker of Light and a believer in the I AM.

Why do you think Mary Magdalene went to the tomb while it was still dark?

What did she find and what did she do?

How did the disciples react? Be sure to include John 20:10 as part of your answer.

What does Mary do next?

What does Mary Magdalene do with what she has learned?

While we do not know for certain any more details about Mary Magdalene's story, I firmly believe that she was among the group mentioned in Acts 1:12-14.

> *All these with one accord were devoting themselves to prayer, together with the women and Mary the mother of Jesus, and his brothers. (Acts 1:14)*

And based on her actions throughout the gospels, Mary Magdalene surely continued as a follower of the Light of the World, sharing her testimony of belief in YHWH the Light with others she encountered.

> *After encountering the Light, she saw things more clearly*
> *and longed for others to have that same experience.*

From the Common Threads: Have you "seen the Light"? How will you **grow and bloom** in your belief of the I AM and share that testimony with others?

Reflectors of Light

Mary Magdalene, Paul, and other followers we have not yet mentioned became reflectors of Light after encountering the I AM, Light of the World. Like Moses, their transformation became a reflection of the I AM's glory (2 Cor. 3:18).

What does Matthew 5:14-16 say is our job?

The Light of the World invites us to participate with Him in sharing the Light, all to His glory. **As reflectors of the I AM's Light, we have a tremendous responsibility.** Therefore, at times, we may feel inadequate to the task or like a less-than-ideal reflector of light. Discouraged by imperfections and torn down by failures, doubts overwhelm the desire to shine. We are not alone in that struggle. And there is hope when we see things clearly.

From the Common Threads: What **thorn** needs to be removed in order to shine His Light?

Paul puts words to our wrestling in 2 Corinthians 4. Allow me to illustrate this point by reading the following verses in reverse order. Maintaining these verses in their context, but looking at them in a different order, we will discover some additional insights and bring other things to light.

> [8] *We are afflicted in every way, but not crushed; perplexed, but not driven to despair;* [9] *persecuted, but not forsaken; struck down, but not destroyed;* [10] *always carrying in the body the death of Jesus, so that the life of Jesus may also be manifested in our bodies.* (2 Cor. 4:8-10)

What happens when we focus on the negative descriptions in 2 Cor. 4:8-10, versus the "but not..." phrases?

Afflicted and broken, the focus can easily be shifted to a victim mentality instead of on the I AM who powerfully works in us. Underline the "but not..." phrases (i.e. "but not crushed") and re-read verses 8 and 9 with that emphasis. What do we see more clearly with that perspective?

Now, back to 2 Corinthians 4:7.

> [7] *But we have this treasure in jars of clay, to show that the surpassing power belongs to God and not to us.*

Clay jars are weak and fragile. It is not about the jar, but rather about what the jar carries inside.

It is not about "I" but rather about the "I AM" in me.

Because when a clay jar has a crack, the broken place is where the light best shines through. **Remember Who is the Light. We are merely reflectors of Him.**

> [5] *For what we proclaim is not ourselves, but Jesus Christ as Lord, with ourselves as your servants for Jesus' sake.* [6] *For God, who said, "Let light shine out of darkness," has shone in our hearts to give the light of the knowledge of the glory of God in the face of Jesus Christ.* (2 Cor. 4:5-6)

This way God gets all the glory! The good news of the gospel—the incarnation of the I AM—is that the Light of the World came down to shatter the darkness and offers us the opportunity to bring others to the Light of truth and hope. He is the Light of Life (John 8:12)!

What thoughts do you have about light, broken clay jars, and the passage in 2 Corinthians 4?

Light is an Invitation

Light is life-giving: Plants, people, animals... anything living requires light in order to survive, especially if it wants to thrive. **While light is vital for physical life, to remain walking in the Light is vital for spiritual life.**

What two things does Jesus ask us to do, according to John 12:35-36?

What is the promise in John 12:36?

What a blessing to walk in the Light and be in relationship with Him! How do we make the most of walking in the light and maintain our walk in the light? Name at least three ways.

Now turn with me to 1 John 1:5-10. What are the blessings of walking in the light?

What is the promise when we confess our sins or "bring them to light"?

The accuser, Satan, dwells in the darkness and reigns there. **The father of lies parades as an angel of light (2 Cor. 11:14) and wants to keep us from bringing anything to light because light is where healing, repentance, and power are found.** Light is transformative and when we confess our sins, the Light of the World overshadows any unrighteousness we may have tried to keep hidden with His perfect righteousness.

What an offer the Light makes and a ministry of Light He has called us to! As Paul paraphrased his commission to the Gentiles in Acts 26:18, he was sent...

to open their eyes, so that they may turn from darkness to light and from the power of Satan to God, that they may receive forgiveness of sins and a place among those who are sanctified by faith in me.

From the Common Threads: What are ways in which an Iron Rose Sister can serve as **iron sharpening iron** and encourage you to **dig deeper** in your relationship with the I AM, walking in the Light as He is the Light?

True Light

Ever been in a cave? You can't even see your hand in front of your face. You feel the darkness. The absence of light is haunting and oppressive. The mere spark of a match to light a small candle dispels the gloom and hope is restored.

However, some people, after growing accustomed to the dimness of the candle, falsely assume that it is adequate light to navigate the cave and therefore remain content in semi-darkness. The shadows play tricks on their minds and the darkness embraces them again providing a false sense of temporary security.

Once lost in a sea of darkness, a distant light can serve as an invitation or a source of fear—a hope of rescue or a terrifying unknown. How does John 3:19-21 describe that phenomenon in a spiritual sense?

Why do we fear the Light?

How can we overcome that fear? What are practical ways to look to the Light, see things more clearly, and believe?

The Light Who Was, Is, and Is to Come

My belief in the I AM, Light of the World, grows when I remember the eternal, never-changing, faithful characteristics of the Light. **When I look to the Light, everything else pales in comparison.**

Did you know that light does not have a shadow? Try it! You can test this by shining a separate light (like a flashlight) on the flame of a tall candle in a dark room. Look at the wall behind the candle. The wax of the candle will have a shadow, but the flame will not.

> *"...God is light, and in him is NO darkness AT ALL"* (1 John 1:5b; emphasis mine)... not even a shadow!

> *"...the Father of lights, with whom there is no variation or shadow due to change"* (James 1:17b). YHWH Light, who was and is and is to come.

> *"And the city has no need of sun or moon to shine on it, for the glory of God gives it light, and its lamp is the Lamb"* (Rev. 21:23). **The I AM, lighting the Way to eternal Light with Him, forever.**

How do these verses about eternal Light inspire you?

> *Whether asked from a place of confusion, despair, lostness, or doubt, the questions of life can be answered by looking to the Light of the World for clarity, hope, direction, and certainty.*

When we walk in the light, as He is in the light, the darkness loses its power over us. Light illuminates the sin that entangles so that we can "fix our eyes on Jesus, the author and perfecter of our faith" (Heb. 12:2).

Our testimony of belief becomes a reflection of the True Light of Life. And as we share our testimonies of the power of that Light, we become an extension of the incarnation and thus invite others to shine His light in their lives. Finally, when we walk in the Light together, His light shines brighter—the embodiment and incarnation of Christ, the I AM.

The I AM, Light of the World, may have brought some **thorns** to light through this chapter. Or maybe you have seen a specific way in which you want to keep **growing** like a blooming rose that looks to the source of Light. Remember: You are not in this alone. Our Iron Rose Sisters are with us on the journey, as **iron sharpening iron**, and even become a part of our testimonies of belief in the Great I AM.

Date of completion: _____

CHAPTER 8

Am I Safe?
The Gate for the Sheep

Therefore Jesus said again, "Very truly I tell you, I am the gate for the sheep.
(John 10:7, NIV)

There is a scene in Disney's *The Lion King*[8] in which the bird, Zazu, entrapped in a carcass cage by the King's brother, Scar, cries, "Let me out! Let me out!" In the very next moment, Timon, the meerkat, runs into the cave where Zazu is trapped, because he is being chased by hyenas. He cries, "Let me in! Let me in!" and squeezes between the bones of the carcass cage to join Zazu. Zazu first looks at Timon like he is crazy, but the approaching hyenas quickly confirm that they are both in the right place—the safe place.

What one animal saw as imprisonment, the other saw as protection; it's all a matter of perspective.

We learn a lot from animals, and not just the talking ones that Walt Disney and other companies use to narrate fairytale stories. Jesus used animals in His parables to make His points applicable to His audience.

---

8 The Lion King (Walt Disney Pictures, 1994).

The birds of the air and the lilies of the field have nothing to worry about, so why should we (Matt. 6:25-34)? The shepherd goes in search for his lost sheep and rejoices as the Father rejoices when we return (Luke 15:1-7).

Sheep are what we, as followers, are most often compared to, throughout the Bible. The prevalence of sheep in the region allowed for rich illustrations and relatable stories.

What do we know about sheep? If you have never seen or worked with sheep, check out a YouTube® video—but only if you will not be distracted!

Sheep are vulnerable. Their minimal intelligence requires total dependence on a shepherd to care for their needs. In John 10, we see a lengthy discourse by the LORD comparing us to sheep.

In the next chapter of this book, we will focus on the I AM, the Good Shepherd and how He cares for His sheep, but for now, we will emphasize how the I AM is the Gate for the Sheep.

When there is a barrier—a wall, a fence, a border—the gate is the place of safe passage. When the Israelites came up against the Red Sea with the Egyptians close on their tails, "safe" was not one of the best words to describe how they felt at that time. The text says they "feared greatly" (Ex. 14:10) and then began to cry out to the LORD.

"But, God...?" Why didn't you leave us in Egypt? "But, God...?" How can you let this happen to me? "But, God...?" Can't you picture them even stomping their feet as they say it, like a spoiled toddler?

On the other hand, if we look at the concept of that phrase at a different point in the story, "But, God..." takes on a completely new meaning.

Circumstances were against them, "But, God..." The enemy was at their heels, "But, God..." There is no way out, "But, God..."

The I AM reveals Himself in amazing ways at times when we are most vulnerable, assuring us that we are safe, protected, secure, and loved, ushering us into safety.

"But, God..." I love that phrase!

For the Israelites that day, He opened a gate in the Red Sea— created a passage on dry land through which they walked. Then, when the enemy followed, attempting to pass through the gate, He shut the door in their faces, so to speak, wiping them from the face of the earth.

"But, God!"

What is a "But, God!" story in your life? A time when the I AM protected you, led you to safety, or lovingly made you feel secure.

These stories are our testimonies of belief in the I AM, the Gate for the sheep.

> *When we doubt and question, "But, God?" may we remember our "But, God!" stories and His forever answer, "I already AM."*

The Purpose of a Gate

A gate may seem like a cold, inanimate object. However, a gate implies relationship. Before we continue, read our central text for this chapter, John 10:1-10.

During the time of Jesus, there were two different types of sheep pens or sheepfolds: one communal with a strong shared gate, the other a makeshift gathering of rocks into a circle in an open field with the shepherd laying down at the entrance as the gate.

In this second instance of a gate, what purpose does the shepherd serve?

How does this help the sheep feel safe?

Whom does the shepherd let in? Whom does he keep out?

Access and Protection: Two of the primary functions of a gate. You grant access to those you love. You protect those you love from those who do not have access. Again, a gate implies relationship.

What (or whom) does the I AM, the Gate for the sheep, grant us access to?

What does the I AM, the Gate for the sheep, protect us from?

Whose Gate is This?

In order to access the apartment where I lived for four years in Caracas, Venezuela, you had to go through two gates, a keyed elevator, and another gate before unlocking my door. These security measures were occasionally annoying, like when lugging as many bags of groceries as I could possibly carry across my arms and fingers. However, most of the time, it offered a measure of protection for a single woman living in a metropolitan city of millions.

The first time I visited Venezuela, I was unaccustomed to the need for that level of security. I also wondered if anonymity was the norm, especially in the small towns. Houses did not have numbers; streets were not labeled.

During an evangelistic campaign in a mid-sized city, I quickly learned that points of reference were much more accurate for returning to a house in order to deliver a Bible correspondence course. Many did not know their address, but a few indications of nearby bread stores and the color of their gate made for a more accurate identification during a later visit.

The bright colors of paint distinguished the gates, one from another, even if they became a faded version of their original brilliance, dulled by the sun and chipped by the keys used to "knock" on the metal gates while hollering out in order to get someone's attention inside the house.

Along a country road in the U.S., a gate at the edge of the road may have a sign indicating who lives at the end of the drive, or the name of the farm.

Across the world, in different shapes and forms, gates and doors are markers of identity. For a shepherd who would lay across a doorless entrance to the sheepfold, he *was* the gate—the incarnation of identity, access, and protection.

With the description of identity in mind, how do you see the I AM as the Gate for the sheep?

The Sheep Gate

Back to John 10:1-10. Did you notice that the I AM declares Himself the Gate for the sheep before He identifies Himself as the Good Shepherd? What does this illustrate or imply?

Let's look at one additional description of Sheep Gates or gates for the sheep, drawing from biblical history. The I AM, in His declaration of identity in John 10 highlights a contrast between the Sheep Gate in Jerusalem (Neh. 3:1, 32) and Himself as the living and eternal Gate for the sheep.

Nehemiah describes the twelve gates of Jerusalem that were constructed in the rebuilding of the wall. The first gate was called the Sheep Gate. This was the one and only door through which sheep and other animals entered. And once they entered, they never left. Their access to the city was for one purpose: sacrifice. **What came in through the Sheep Gate never went back out.**

Therefore, when Jesus explains that He is the Gate for the sheep, what is the significance of what He promises in John 10:9?

Additionally, what is promised in John 10:10?

Thinking of I AM, the Gate for the sheep, describe the abundant life He offers. Give three specific examples of what the abundant life is or isn't.

From the Common Threads: What is an aspect of the I AM, or of the abundant life He offers, that you will **grow and bloom** in your belief of?

Abundant Life of Grace and Truth

Self-assured in their course of action, the scribes and Pharisees thought they were living an abundant life; yet what it was abounding in was self-righteousness. In John 8:1-11, we see an example of their perceived superiority.

According to John 8:6, what was the intention of the scribes and Pharisees?

Describe how the woman felt.

How do we see the qualities of the I AM, the Gate for the sheep, in this story? Be sure to include manifestations of access, protection, and identity for the woman, as well as for the scribes and Pharisees.

The Pharisees brought the woman caught in adultery as a sheep for slaughter. Yet YHWH offered her a way out—life instead of sacrifice for others' sins.

> *As the Gate for the sheep, the I AM promises*
> *protection for the vulnerable, access for the outcast, and*
> *a transformed identity for those that others only see as sinners.*

What facet of the I AM's promise speaks to your current circumstances? Do you truly believe in the Gate's answer: "I *already* AM" the fulfillment of that promise?

Another way of phrasing it, the Pharisees brought the woman caught in adultery to the Sheep Gate for sacrifice, but instead, encountered the life-giving Gate for the sheep, who introduced each of them to grace and truth.

I won't ask if you have ever led someone to the Sheep Gate in a spirit of condemnation... Let's rather focus on how we can bring others to the I AM, the Gate for the sheep. Name at least one way in which you can introduce someone to the protector of the vulnerable, giver of abundant life, and access to the Father—the Gate for the sheep.

Another Vulnerable Woman

No one wants to be known for her biggest mistake... Life learners recognize that no one has it all together. We encounter new challenges. We recognize that our way isn't actually the only way to do something. For example, did you know there's more than one way to burn a piece of toast?

College students are at a pivotal point in their lives when life lessons can be especially harsh. Mistakes can have long-term repercussions or consequences, much graver than a burnt piece of toast.

With those larger-than-life choices, grace and forgiveness can usher in the opportunity to learn from those mistakes moving forward. In contrast, condemnation can serve as a black mark on their identity—perceived to be the filter through which others see them.

While working in campus ministry, one of the students in the group made some poor decisions and took some actions that morphed into a personal attack against me. She became the victim and I was the supposed aggressor for having attempted to lovingly correct her. Rallying others in her corner, many came to her defense, not knowing the entire story.

It was not my story to tell. Unwilling to divulge things shared confidentially, even if it meant saving my own hide, I was left with only one option: turn the other cheek.

Far from saintly in my behavior and recognizing my part in the situation, I crumbled before God; mortified by how my words had contributed to the situation this student was reacting to. The mature part of me realized that she was attacking the messenger who had done a poor job of communicating God's message. However, the vulnerable part of me was wounded and defeated.

Crying out to God, I felt the weight of the part I had played. Moreover, I was fearful of the next barrage of attacks from the group of people the student had convinced to champion her cause.

Bracing myself, expecting a reprimand from God and anticipating repercussions in my job, I clung to the verses of promise in which the I AM keeps me safe and protected (Prov. 18:10), does not abandon or forsake me (Josh. 1:5), and the blessings that come when I forgive (Matt. 6:14-15). Graced by the Spirit's gentle reminders, the following phrase came to mind, "No one wants to be known for their biggest mistake."

Still in a vulnerable state, I knew forgiveness was something we all needed: **freedom from an identity defined by our mistakes**. Parables reminded me that there is no "bigger" or "smaller" sin (Matt. 18:21-35). Even if reconciliation was impossible, forgiveness was necessary. Why would I deny her the blessing I also longed for? I could not let her identity, in my mind, be dominated by her personal attack against me. She was more than this attack. **God saw me as more than my mistakes.** The same grace I wanted for myself had to be extended to her as well.

Years later, the truth came out and my reputation was somewhat redeemed by the revelation, although no one spoke about it directly. **Again, none of us want to be reminded of our mistakes, nor do we want to recognize when the mistakes of others lead us to make mistakes of our own.** "Let he who is without sin..."

From the Common Threads: What **thorn** of sin is hindering your relationship with the I AM or with others?

Protected, Safe, or Saved?

I am my own worst enemy. James 1:14-15 reminds me that my own desires are the primary source of my undoing, if not kept in check. Thoughts, words, actions, attacks, temptations, suffering, oneself...

What do you most want to feel protected from (may be the thorn you just listed)?

What does it mean to be safe? What does it mean to be saved? Is there a difference? Explain.

Promises Fulfilled through the Gate

In closing, make note of the following verses, writing out the promises of protection, safety, access, or identity in each. And stay tuned for some of the remaining chapters in which the I AM restates and solidifies these truths yet again.

Job 5:11

Psalm 4:8

Psalm 91:14

Proverbs 18:10

John 17:11

The I AM, the Gate for the Sheep, affirms that you are safe and offers the opportunity to be saved. He grants access to the Father, protects us from the enemy, and ushers us into an abundant life through our identity in Him. **Welcomed into the sheepfold, we are called to invite others as well.**

How has your belief in the LORD, the Gate for the Sheep, grown this week?

.

From the Common Threads: Ways in which an Iron Rose Sister can serve as **iron sharpening iron** and encourage you to **dig deeper** in your relationship with the I AM:

A verse, word of encouragement, or reminder of the I AM:

Date of completion: _____

CHAPTER 9

Does Anyone Truly Know Me?
The Good Shepherd

"I am the good shepherd. The good shepherd lays down his life for the sheep."

"I am the good shepherd; I know my sheep and my sheep know me—"
(John 10:11, 14)

A phone call with my college roommate reminds me how much we learned each other's quirks while sharing a dorm room. A quote from Mom affirms that I have known her and listened to her voice my entire life. Working alongside my dad and anticipating the next thing he needs for a project indicates how well I know him. And ordering two waters without ice before my friend arrives for lunch suggests this is not our first meal shared together.

Each of those people have more than a few stories that reflect how well they know me as well. **There is a unique comfort found in spending time with those with whom you share a history.** Shared experiences bond us, creating memories and connections that can last a lifetime.

As the oldest of four girls, the bonds of sisterhood and intimate knowledge of one another is a blessing I have experienced since age three. Although we have each had different experiences as adults, living in different cities (and countries!), the family bonds remain.

A few of my friends have adopted themselves into the family and we welcome them! One such friend is surprised, every single time we get together, and comments with genuine shock, "I can't believe how well you know me!" We have been through tough times together, seeing each other at our worst; we have rejoiced together through the joyous times. Her daughter once said, "I think you know my mom better than she knows herself!"

We chuckled at the comment and reminisced about how freeing it is to be with someone who truly knows you. There is no mask, no putting on a show, no pretenses, no confusion... Don't get me wrong, there continue to be miscommunications and occasional hurt feelings. We are not perfect! However, there is a peace in **being seen and known**. The I AM sees us. The Good Shepherd knows us.

> *There is a comfort in being accepted as you are,*
> *while being cheered on to be the best version of yourself.*

I AM the Good Shepherd

In the previous chapter, we explored how Jesus declared Himself to be the Gate for the sheep from John 10. In this chapter, we will study the surrounding verses in which Jesus declares, "I AM the Good Shepherd."

Turn to John 10:1-6, 11-18.

According to different translations of John, at least four types of people are described as what the shepherd is not. List as many as you can find, referencing additional versions of the Bible as well (John 10:1, 5, 12).

How would you describe these types of people and how do they compare and contrast with the shepherd?

In light of the many references to sheep and shepherds in the Bible, we tend to glorify that career path. Yet, the job of shepherd is no easy task. Sheep stink. They are dumb. They require constant care and attention. While possibly a great job for introverts who like to sing or play an instrument to calm the sheep, the profession is a huge risk to your life because of the lions and tigers and bears, oh my! Okay, maybe not the same animals that Dorothy feared, but there were many ferocious animals that attacked the flock. The shepherd's job was to protect the sheep and lead them beside still waters, among other things...

Turn to Psalm 23 and David's description of the Good Shepherd. List seven things the shepherd does for the sheep.

Who does David call his shepherd? Hint: Pay attention to capital letters!

As a reminder, what does LORD mean (vs. Lord)? Feel free to look back at chapter 3 for a reminder.

Yes! YHWH, LORD, the I AM was, is, and always will be the Good Shepherd!

How does Isaiah 40:11 describe the Good Shepherd?

In John 10:1-18, how does the incarnation of the I AM describe Himself as a shepherd, the Good Shepherd?

And what are we promised that the Good Shepherd will be in Revelation 7:17?

Looking back at the list of things the shepherd does for the sheep from Psalm 23 and the descriptions of the Good Shepherd who was, is, and is to come (in Isaiah, John, and Revelation)... How does the Good Shepherd do those things for us today? Describe at least four ways you have experienced the Good

Shepherd in your own life (additional space available in Notes/Testimonies section).

The Good Shepherd's work in your life is another part of your testimony of belief!

What the Good Shepherd Looks At

The Good Shepherd sees with a different perspective than the world does.

Remember when Moses ran away from Egypt? What did he become? Yep, a shepherd (Ex. 3:1). Yet, I AM had a bigger plan for Moses than tending wooly animals. Moses, whose name means "drawn out" or "delivered" was not the deliverer. **Rather his job was to point others to YHWH, the Deliverer, the Good Shepherd, who truly loved and cared for His sheep.**

Moses drew from his experience as a shepherd to help him guide the Israelites to food, water, and shelter. Ultimately, he was asked to guide them to the Good Shepherd, the Bread of Life, the Living Water, the Gate for the sheep, and the other manifestations of who the I AM is.

YHWH used another shepherd in the Bible to draw others to Him. David, who wrote Psalm 23, had a career as a shepherd until the I AM was ready to use his shepherding skills for a more eternal impact.

1 Samuel 16:1-13 tells the story of David's anointing. What were Jesse (David's father), David's brothers and even the prophet Samuel expecting? What eyes were they looking with?

What was the LORD looking for? (1 Sam. 13:14; Acts 13:22)

What does the I AM see that man doesn't?

Who the Good Shepherd Sees

God loves the outcast, the forgotten, the one that feels unseen, unknown, left out, or not taken into account.

El Roi is the Hebrew for "The God who Sees."

Genesis 16 is when we are first introduced to this characteristic of God. Read the entire chapter and answer the following questions.

Who was Hagar?

What made Hagar feel unseen? What other words would you use to describe how Hagar felt?

Who *did* see Hagar?

What did the I AM do to affirm and "see" Hagar?

Bible stories illustrate how the LORD sees His people

The I AM sees the beloved Rachel who could not have children (Gen. 29-30).

The I AM sees the less-desirable Leah who still could not win her husband's favor with six sons (Gen. 29-30).

The I AM sees the prostitute Rahab who turned her life around after protecting the spies (Josh. 2; Heb. 11:31; James 2:25).

The I AM sees the embittered Naomi (Ruth 1), Tamar who was forgotten (Gen. 38), and Dinah who was raped (Gen. 34).

The I AM sees the seeker in the Samaritan woman (John 4), the servant in Phoebe (Rom. 16:1), and the woman suffering from a chronic illness (Luke 8:43-48).

The I AM has never stopped seeing His people. Complete the next four sentences, following the same model as the previous sentences. Come up with two more Bible stories for the first two, then add two stories of your own or of others you have personally witnessed the I AM seeing and knowing, as the Good Shepherd.

(Bible story) The I AM sees

(Bible story) The I AM sees

(Today) The I AM sees

(Today) The I AM sees

The Good Shepherd Knows

The Good Shepherd knows and sees each of us,
longing for us to draw close to Him.

Reflection from John 10:14: Do I believe the Good Shepherd knows me? If not, have I allowed myself to be His own?

Read the following verses and make note of how the Good Shepherd knows you, what He knows about you, and how much He wants to know you more.

Psalm 139

Luke 12:6-7

John 10:3 & Isaiah 40:26

Did you know that there are more than 1,000,000,000,000,000,000,000 stars in the known universe? That is more than 1 billion trillion stars. Abraham likely had no idea how many descendants he would have when God promised him more than the innumerable stars in the sky (Gen. 15:5). Yet, as Isaiah 40:26 affirms, YHWH knows each of them by name and His Presence is there, longing for relationship with each and every one.

At the end of Isaiah 40:26, the phrase, "Not one is missing," reminds me of one more sheep story: Luke 15:1-7.

What do we learn about the Good Shepherd from the Luke 15 parable?

According to John 10:11-18, how does the I AM begin and end His description of the Good Shepherd? What does the Good Shepherd do for His sheep?

> *The Good Shepherd and the sheep have a relationship of trust, reliance, and intimacy. Knowing the Good Shepherd allows me to believe Him.*

The nearness of our relationship allows me to recognize His voice and be drawn to Him (John 10:3, 4, 16). Yet, there are others that are not of His fold that do not yet know His voice. **One of our blessings and responsibilities is to share our testimony of belief in the Good Shepherd, inviting others to hear and come to know His voice.**

As A. W. Tozer stated it, we want others to know *"that God is here and that He is speaking."*[9] The challenge is that we may be the only voice someone else hears, pointing them to the Good Shepherd. It is our burden, our joy, and our responsibility to live out the incarnation of the I AM, both individually, and as a church, in the lives of others. But can we do so if we don't know the Good Shepherd's voice?

Knowing the Good Shepherd's Voice

My Grandpa had sheep when my dad and his sister moved in with them. As foster children aged 15 and 13 respectively, they were blessed to be taken in by a distantly related Christian couple who my sisters and I grew up knowing as Grandpa and Grandma. Never having had children of their own, they saw the opportunity to make a tremendous impact in the lives of my father and aunt.

---

9 A. W. Tozer, *The Pursuit of God* (Chicago: Moody Publishers, 2015), 81.

Countless stories on the farm could be told, but in a brief interview with my dad, he shared, "I did not grow up around sheep, but I was amazed that the sheep came when Grandpa called them. When we would go to the sheep, he would call them with a certain sound, and they came running. When I first tried to imitate his sound, they could tell the difference and would only come when he called. The sheep knew him and didn't know me. After months and months of trying, I learned how to imitate the sound and the sheep would come when I called. I learned from a master shepherd how to call and take care of the sheep. I think that's why they started coming when they heard my voice too... To this day, I remember distinctly and can still make the sound that he made. And, as you know, I learned a lot more than sheep-calling from Grandpa."

What do we learn about recognizing the Good Shepherd's voice?

How do we hear the Good Shepherd's voice? And how do we distinguish it from other voices in our lives?

Finally, how do we echo the Good Shepherd's voice, as my dad learned from my Grandpa, in order to point others to the Good Shepherd?

Common Threads

In Hebrew, *Yahweh Rohi* means LORD, my Shepherd, the **One Who feeds and leads.** The Good Shepherd's care, guidance, and provision speak to His relationship with His sheep. I AM, the Good Shepherd, lays down His life for His sheep that we might all become a part of His fold. What a humbling reminder of the depth of love the Good Shepherd has for us, His treasured sheep!

A name or characteristic of the I AM that you will **grow and bloom** in your belief of:

Removing the **thorn** of a flawed perspective or distracted focus:

Ways in which an Iron Rose Sister can serve as **iron sharpening iron** and encourage you to **dig deeper** in your relationship with the I AM:

A verse, word of encouragement, or reminder of the I AM:

Date of completion: _____

CHAPTER 10

Where do I find hope?
The Resurrection and the Life

Jesus said to her, "I am the resurrection and the life. Whoever believes in me, though he die, yet shall he live, and everyone who lives and believes in me shall never die. Do you believe this?" (John 11:25-26)

I'm waiting...

The five-year-old waits for Christmas morning. The mom waits for a full night's sleep. The grandpa waits to see his grandkids again.

The student waits for the semester to be over. The employee waits for a promotion. The hard-worker waits for a vacation. The stressed-out wife waits for this season of life to pass.

We are all waiting.

We wait in anticipation of what is to come. And most waiting is filled with hope and excited expectations. However, the patient that waits for news from the doctor may prefer to extend the waiting and not hear that her cancer is back. The young wife who has been trying for years to get pregnant is not looking forward to another month of waiting to see if their dreams will be realized.

We are all waiting.

Describe a time in which you hoped and waited with expectation for something (e.g. a bicycle for your birthday, a visit from a friend, a graduation, a new job...)

Now describe a time in which you observed someone else hoping and waiting for something in eager expectation (No names!). What was it like watching them? Were you excited? Jealous? Dismissive? Did their hopes and dreams match yours?

A guy I was dating in my younger years told me the story of how his dad had filled him with anticipation for a most-excellent Christmas present. His dad would give no hints at what it was, but that it was "the best gift you could imagine." Fast forward to the Christmas while we were dating... In order to create anticipation for the gift he was going to get me, he used the same phrase and no other hints. "It will be the best gift you can imagine," he would repeat with a teasing grin.

I waited and hoped, expecting that it was going to be an engagement ring—the promise of his love and our future life together. However, my Christmas present that year was not an engagement ring. The best gift *I* could imagine and the best gift *he* could imagine were very different.

What happens when our hopes and dreams are not fulfilled? What does the expression "mourning expectations" mean?

People fail us. Our expectations are not met. Things do not always turn out as we would hope. We wait for something that doesn't happen. And we can become discouraged and distrusting when we have suffered from unfulfilled promises in our past. **Trust issues creep in and our tainted lens distorts our perspective on the I AM's faithfulness or the ways in which we believe in the hope He provides.**

Have you experienced a time in which YHWH's promises to do beyond what we can ask or imagine did not match what you hoped, expected, or were waiting for? How did this positively or negatively impact your belief in Him?

Wait, Hope, Expect

You may have noticed a combination of the words "wait," "hope," and "expect," throughout the aforementioned stories and questions. There is intentionality in the interchangeable nature of those three words in English.

Did you know that there is one only verb each in Spanish (*esperar*) and in Hebrew (*qavah*) that are typically translated three ways into English—wait, hope, or expect?

While each of those three words has their own nuances or unique connotations in context, let's think about how much greater our hope would be if we wait, hope, *and* expect in the Lord.

Micah 7:7 gives a good example of all three concepts in the same verse:

> But as for me, I watch in hope for the LORD, I wait for God my Savior; my God will hear me.

If I "watch in *hope*," I *expect* that His promises will be fulfilled.

I *"wait* for God my Savior," not knowing the timeframe, but *expecting* with *hope*.

And I believe, *expecting* that "He will hear me."

What a blessing!

How does the connection between the words wait, hope, and expect, change your understanding of our belief in the I AM?

Let's look at two more verses, inserting the three possible translations for new insight. Based on whichever translation of the Bible you are using, Isaiah 40:31 may use the word "wait" or "hope." And now you know why some translators choose those different words!

Write out the first sentence of Isaiah 40:31 inserting each of the three words: wait, hope, expect (the first one is done for you). As you do this exercise, a different image may come to mind from this verse for each of the words used. Feel free to draw it out as we expand our understanding of these promises of God.

Wait: *They who <u>wait for</u> the LORD shall renew their strength.*

Hope:

Expect:

Now do the same for Psalm 31:24.

Wait:

Hope:

Expect:

What does this exercise bring to light about the characteristics of the I AM and the hope we place in Him? How is this hope connected to belief?

From the Common Threads: What is a promise or characteristic of the I AM that you will **grow and bloom** in your belief of, through hope?

Hope in the Resurrection

> *My belief in the hope of the resurrection is impossible without a belief in the resurrection.*

Re-read that sentence and then write it out below.

Reflection: Do I truly believe in the resurrection?

Martha was forced to answer this question when her expectations for how Jesus would take care of her brother were not met. Martha didn't want her brother to die, yet her hope in the resurrection sustained her, when death became the harsh reality within her family. However, we learn, along with Martha, that her initial understanding and belief in the resurrection were incomplete...

Turn with me to John 11 in order to read this story from her perspective—the context for this chapter's I AM declaration.

According to John 11:1-16, describe Jesus' relationship with Martha and her siblings.

Martha is often criticized for her role and her mistaken focus in Luke 10:38-42. Yet, in this story, Martha is the one to whom Jesus proclaims His identity! Paying special attention to Martha's interactions with Jesus, read John 11:17-27.

In John 11:20, we see that Martha did not wait until Jesus came to the house, but rather she went and met him. Picture yourself on that dusty road between Bethany and Jerusalem. This well-traversed path likely had other travelers and vendors that Martha passed on her way to meet Jesus. Think of the smells, the sounds, the gritty, rocky ground under well-worn sandals... Did Martha grab an extra cloak before she ran out the door, pushing her way through the crowd of mourners accompanying her and her sister?

Now that you are there with Martha in the moment, describe the circumstances surrounding this interaction between friends in John 11:21-27. What kind of things would be going on in Martha's head throughout their conversation?

Stay in that moment with Martha... In the midst of her grief, the noise of the street, and everything else, the I AM reveals Himself as the Resurrection and the Life.

What is the significance of the I AM statement Jesus shares with Martha (the meaning of what He says and the significance of revealing it to a woman)?

How would you have reacted if Jesus told you directly, "I AM the Resurrection and the Life"?

Martha responds with belief, even before Jesus reveals who He is. Describe what Martha believes before and after the I AM statement.

Martha is not the primary character in John 11:28-37, but there we find critical elements of the story and how Jesus reveals Himself as the Resurrection and the Life. What do we observe about Mary and some of the other Jews?

Now, for the final portion of Martha's part in this story... Read John 11:38-40 and notice the conversation between Martha and Jesus. Based on the previous encounters, what do you think was the tone of this part of their conversation? How did Jesus respond to her doubts?

In John 11:41-45, what does Jesus affirm is His purpose and His identity?

How does the I AM's purpose and identity inform our purpose and identity?

Belief in a Hope that Never Fails

In John 11:4, before Martha enters the scene, Jesus explained to His disciples the purpose of the rest of the events over the next few days. What was it?

How many times in John 11 do we see the word "believe"? What do these occurrences reveal about the I AM and those who saw what He did?

What would be the highlights from the testimonies of belief, as shared by Martha, Mary, the disciples, the rest of the Jews, or even Lazarus, from that day? Choose one of the characters and make notes about how they might have shared their testimony of belief from that day.

Can you imagine Lazarus' testimony? Not many people experience that kind of a revelation of the I AM as the Resurrection and the Life?! What is the closest you have come to observing a resurrection? A resurrected friendship or marriage... being restored to health... financial peace... a transformed life?

How do we arrive at our belief in the resurrection? What brings us to our testimonies of belief in the hope of the resurrection?

Coming at it from a different direction, using the Common Threads: What **thorn** is hindering your belief or your hope in the resurrection?

Read Romans 5:1-5 and Psalm 25:1-7 in order to answer the following questions: What kind of hope are Paul and David describing? Where does hope come from or how is it developed?

How have you experienced hope and belief growing through struggles? (Rom. 8:24-25 may provide additional insight for why this happens.) Please be sure to share a testimony of belief in the I AM through hope in the midst of trials... maybe a time when He felt unseen.

Name three specific ways to hold onto hope in difficult circumstances (could be a stressful day, a complicated relationship, a challenging situation...)

> *My hope in the I AM will never be put to shame because the Resurrection and the Life always was, always is, and always will be.*

Through the Common Threads, we are spurring one another on to love and good works, we are reminding each other of the hope we have in Christ, and we are challenging each other to share that hope with others—all together, as Iron Rose Sisters!

> [23] *Let us hold fast the confession of our hope without wavering, for he who promised is faithful.* [24] *And let us consider how to stir up one another to love and good works,* [25] *not neglecting to meet together, as is the habit of some, but encouraging one another, and all the more as you see the Day drawing near.* (Heb. 10:23-25)

From the Common Threads: What are ways in which an Iron Rose Sister can remind you of the hope of the resurrection? How can you each serve as **iron sharpening iron** and encourage one another to **dig deeper** in your relationships with the I AM?

I Hope, I Wish, I Want

In Scripture, we learn of a host of the faithful who waited and never got to see what was promised:

> *"And all these, though commended through their faith, did not receive what was promised, since God had provided something better for us, that apart from us they should not be made perfect"* (Heb. 11:39-40).

When I read these verses, I find hope in God's perspective that is bigger than my own. Everyone's perspectives on hopes, wishes, and wants are unique. Different cultures, contexts, and life circumstances bring to light distinct perspectives on hope. We observe others whose prayers are answered, hopes are fulfilled, or in contrast, the injustices of the world that shatter our hopes.

> *"Hope," wrote N.T. Wright, "is what you get when you suddenly realize that a different worldview is possible, a worldview in which the rich, the powerful, and the unscrupulous do not after all have the last word. The same*

worldview shift that is demanded by the resurrection of Jesus is the shift that will enable us to change the world.[10]

True hope is found only in the I AM, the Resurrection and the Life!

> *When I ask myself: Is my hope found in the answer to my prayers or in the One who is the answer? His response is "I already AM!"*

The Eternal Hope of a Resurrected Life

What is the greatest hope we have in Christ?

The entire chapter of 1 Corinthians 15 describes various facets and applications of the resurrection. For the purposes of our focus on the I AM as the Resurrection and the Life, we will highlight only the beginning and the end of Paul's discourse.

1 Corinthians 15:1-11 provides an excellent summary of the gospel—the good news. Summarize the gospel, the good news, in your own words, using 1 Corinthians 15 as a model.

Describe the hope found in the gospel.

---

10 As quoted by Rachel Held Evans, *Inspired* (Nashville: Nelson Books, 2018), 185.

Therefore, if we have been united with Christ in His resurrection (Rom. 6:1-4) and have been born again into a living hope (1 Peter 1:3), we are already participating in the eternal life, as promised in Him.

> *In order for there to be a resurrection, there must first be a death. Yet 1 Corinthians 15:53-58 affirms that even though death is unavoidable, it does not have to be eternal.*

And when we hold fast, unshifting in the hope of the good news gospel (Col. 1:23), we also recognize it is intended to be passed on to others (Col. 1:3-12, 23-27; 1 Cor. 15:11).

Our personal testimonies of belief in the resurrection, and our incarnation of a resurrected life, become an invitation to others of the eternal hope found in the I AM.

How will you embody the hope of the resurrection through your testimony of belief this week? Be specific!

Therefore I Will Hope

In conclusion, turn with me to Lamentations 3:21-24.

Our hope and His mercies are new every morning because I AM *already* **is, was, and will be the Resurrection and the Life. Amen!**

On your own, and also when you gather with your Iron Rose Sisters, sing *"The Steadfast Love of the Lord,"* taken directly from Lamentations 3.

And as we share in the eternal hope of the I AM, the Resurrection and the Life, may we hold fast to the confession of our hope!

Finally, my prayer for you this week comes from Romans 15:13, *"May the God of hope fill you with all joy and peace in believing, so that by the power of the Holy Spirit you may abound in hope."*

Date of completion: _____

CHAPTER 11

Whom do I believe?
The Way, the Truth,
and the Life

Jesus said to him, "I am the way, and the truth, and the life.
No one comes to the Father except through me. (John 14:6)

A talented woodworker in a small town in Venezuela came recommended by many. The glowing endorsements warranted a four-hour drive to Quibor from the capital, Caracas, where a friend and I lived. We were in search of high quality, handmade, unique gifts from Venezuela and knew that if we went to the source, we could find better prices than second-hand vendors in the big city.

Determined to make it there and back in one day, we departed before the sun came up, one Saturday morning. However, we did not account for the time it would take to locate the talented woodworker... A lack of street signs and house numbers was typical for this part of the country. So, once we made it to Quibor, confident we were on the correct side of town, we rolled down the windows and began to ask people in the street if they knew of the talented woodworker whose shop was in the back of his house. (I have since forgotten the name of his shop.)

Every single person we asked for directions had a tremendous desire to help us. But only one or two of the more than a dozen people we talked to knew how to tell us where to go.

Nearly at the point of giving up, we met a young man who knew exactly who we were seeking. On this scorching-hot day, he patiently walked next to our car the last few blocks in order to ensure that we arrived at the carpenter's house. Once we arrived, met the artist, and saw his handiwork, we were left with no doubt that our journey had been worth it.

As we began our return trip home, we wondered if there had been a more direct way to arrive at his shop. However, the beautiful carpentry in each of the pieces we purchased allowed the stress of having been lost to fade. We were even able to chuckle at the number of people who pointed us in the totally wrong direction!

Years later, as I have reflected on that day's experience, the spiritual application of this story has become more apparent.

In light of our key verse for the chapter, John 14:6, what lessons do you draw from this illustrative story?

Everyone Has an Opinion, Only God's Matters

"All roads lead to Rome." "There are many spokes on the wheel that all lead to God." Many famous individuals propose a variation on these expressions in defense of the panoply of religions across the world.

How do you talk with someone who believes that lie?

Why is it hard to accept the absolute truth that there is only One Way, One Truth, and One Life?

From the Common Threads: What **thorn** needs to be removed in order for you to fully believe in the Way, the Truth, and the Life?

A Comfort or a Confrontation

Through conversation and Bible study with a variety of women over the years, I have observed a distinct difference in their reactions to John 14:6.

Why is the I AM statement that He is the Way, the Truth, and the Life a comfort to some and a confrontation to others? What makes the difference in our reactions?

Living the Life

The life of a Christian is not a perfect life, but it is promised to be an abundant life filled with love, joy, peace, patience, kindness, goodness, faithfulness, gentleness, and self-control (a.k.a. the fruit of the Spirit, Gal. 5:22-23). Through the support of a Christian family, we share in the hope of heaven and many of the other promises of God.

We long for "the life," but forget that *He* is the Life, not the "ideal life" as we want to live it here on earth.

We get the order backwards. We go after "the life" we think we want, forgetting that the Way to Truth leads us to True Life.

"Give me the life I want! Oh, wait. You mean I have to accept only One Truth and One Way? Well.... Okay, then give me the Jesus that always sings "Jesus loves me." Oh, wait. You mean I have to accept His commands and follow His steps (the Truth and the Way) in order to get the Jesus Life?"

A. W. Tozer expresses it this way: *"Much of our difficulty as seeking Christians stems from our unwillingness to take God as He is and adjust our lives accordingly."*[11]

What is your reaction to the A.W. Tozer quote and the concept of those who want "the life" without the Way or the Truth?

From the Common Threads: What is a facet of the I AM that you want to **grow and bloom** in your belief of?

---

[11] A. W. Tozer, *The Pursuit of God* (Chicago: Moody Publishers, 2015), 105.

The Forever Life

The comfort of knowing and believing in the Way, the Truth, and the Life become another element of our testimony of belief—one that we are honored with the privilege of sharing with others. We have the opportunity to invite others into the eternal life way of living that we confidently step into through belief.

The promise of eternal life is awesome, especially since it means spending eternity with God! But did you know that eternal life doesn't start with physical death, rather we partake of eternal life from the point of our spiritual death through baptism (Rom. 6:1-4).

The terms "life" and "eternal life" are often interchanged in the gospel of John, as well as his later letters, 1, 2, and 3 John.

> *The eternal life that is promised is not just about heaven.*

1 John 5:6-13 provides great confidence of eternal life as an inseparable facet of life in the Son.

And while we have celebrated our testimonies of belief throughout this book, John reminds us that "God's testimony is greater" and that it is *His* testimony that we have within us (1 John 5:9-10). The Spirit testifies to this truth (1 John 5:6). Our testimonies are a reflection and an incarnation of His testimony!

What is God's testimony in 1 John 5:11-12?

The Truth in the Word

The Word, who became flesh and dwelt among us (John 1:14), not only speaks truth, but He embodies truth. **The incarnation of the I AM is Truth, which means that the Truth, as with God, is never-**

changing (**Heb. 13:8**). The I AM, who was, and is, and is to come is faithful, dependable, and true.

What does it mean for your everyday life that Truth is unchanging?

The Word of God, as written in the pages of the Bible, is equally unchanging. The Truth of the Word powerfully cuts through Satan's lies, just as Jesus demonstrated when He was tempted in the desert (Matt. 4:1-11; Luke 4:1-13). An entire interactive Bible study book is dedicated to the practical ways in which we can combat Satan's lies that attack us in very personal ways: *Who Has the Last Word? Cutting through Satan's Lies with the Truth of God's Word*, written by me. That book, a blank Lie-Truth Chart as presented in its pages, and other resources are available through our ministry website: www.IronRoseSister.com.

Gracious Leadership for Finding the One Way

Not everyone has a pioneering spirit. Families who ventured into the Wild West were uncertain what awaited them, but they soldiered on believing in the promise of what lay ahead. Stories and rumors made it difficult to discern what was true or false. Earlier explorers who charted maps and blazed trails made it easier for others who came later to follow the beaten path.

> *When it comes to knowing which way to go, it is much easier to follow the path of someone who has been there or to follow someone else's lead.*

The Israelites, upon leaving Egypt, did not display a pioneering spirit. They had grown accustomed to their previous life and often complained along the journey, as we have explored in previous chapters.

How does the LORD lead the way for His people in Exodus 13:21-22 and direct them in Exodus 40:34-38?

In Nehemiah 9, we see a reference to this same part of the Exodus story. In that chapter, Nehemiah summarizes many of the parallels we have seen between Exodus and John.

Here is Nehemiah 9 in context: After returning to Jerusalem from exile in Babylon, in order to rebuild the wall, Nehemiah, along with Ezra the scribe, facilitate the reading of the Law. Then, being convicted by what is read, the Israelites spend a day reading from the Book of the Law, confessing their sins, and worshipping the LORD their God.

> *Stand up and bless the LORD your God from everlasting to everlasting. Blessed be your glorious name, which is exalted above all blessing and praise. (Neh. 9:5b)*

In celebration of who the LORD is and what He has done for His people, they recount many of the same aspects of the Exodus story that we have studied in this book.

In the summary of the Exodus story, as retold in Nehemiah 9:6-25, what foreshadowing do we see for the incarnation of YHWH through the I AM statements in John 14:6 (the Way, the Truth, and the Life)? Did you notice any other manifestations of the I AM incarnate foreshadowed here? (*addl. space on next page and final page of chapter*)

The story does not end in Nehemiah 9:25. What happens in verses 25-38?

Did you notice the multiple references to God's mercies and steadfast love (Neh. 9:27-33)? What role do these facets of the I AM play in our journey along the Way?

Whom Do You Follow?

Jesus, The I AM incarnate also left us an example, that we should follow in His steps (1 Pet. 2:21). Have you ever been invited to follow someone's example? How did you feel about it? What made the person easy or hard to follow?

What does 1 Corinthians 3:4-9 teach about following others?

While working with the Missions Ministry at the North Atlanta Church of Christ, I was invited to be part of a bilingual team moving to Denver, Colorado, in order to work with one English-speaking church plant and also work toward establishing several Spanish-speaking church plants across the city. In Denver, at that time, over 33% of the population was Spanish-speaking. Yet there was no Hispanic Church of Christ or Latino Ministry in the Denver metro area!

Inspired by the challenge and the team that was forming, I considered the possibility of joining them. Former missionary to Venezuela, Bob Brown, my mentor and boss at the time, encouraged me to go. However, I was hesitant... Part of my reluctance was that I knew that some people would say that I was just going in order to follow Bob, his wife, Kelly, and their family.

Wrestling over my decision, one afternoon, in Bob's office, we animatedly discussed the pros and cons of me moving to Denver. I finally admitted that one of my biggest hindrances was that I didn't want people to think that I was following him, a man. I wanted it to be clear that I was following Christ because He is the only One we are to follow.

Undaunted by my accusing statements, Bob responded, "You should read 1 Corinthians 11:1."

Quick with my retort, I answered, "I have read it! Many times! And I have a problem with that verse. And what about 1 Corinthians 3 that warns against following even Paul or Apollos?!"

He then challenged me to re-read both of the passages (1 Cor. 3 and 1 Cor. 11:1) until I made peace with the verses, which I did, especially when I focused on the second half of 1 Corinthians 11:1.

Using one of my favorite practices for Bible study, we will look at multiple versions of the Bible for a richer, deeper and broader understanding of the text. Underline the second half of each of the following versions of 1 Corinthians 11:1 below.

Be ye followers of me, even as I also am of Christ. (KJV)

Follow me as I follow Christ. (MEV)

Be imitators of me, as I am of Christ. (ESV)

Follow my example, as I follow the example of Christ. (NIV)

What is your understanding of 1 Corinthians 11:1?

A valuable lesson was learned through extensive prayer and study of 1 Corinthians. I began to value more deeply the relationships in my life that model the Christian walk. **Focusing on the Way, the Truth, and the Life allows us to cheer one another on in the journey, while providing personal and practical examples for our daily life.**

The definition of an Iron Rose Sister personifies that kind of relationship. None of us are perfect—far from it! Yet, through our common belief in Christ, we grow and bloom together as iron sharpening iron.

From the Common Threads: How can your Iron Rose Sisters encourage and challenge you in your belief of the I AM as the Way, the Truth, and the Life? What are ways in which an Iron Rose Sister can serve as **iron sharpening iron** and encourage you to **dig deeper** in your relationship with the I AM?

A verse, word of encouragement, or reminder of the I AM:

> *If we know the I AM, we know the Way and can avoid the detours.*
>
> *If we know the I AM, we know the Truth*
> *and can easily recognize the lies.*
>
> *If we know the I AM, we know the Life and can ignore the shadows.*

Date of completion: _____

CHAPTER 12

Where Do I Go from Here? The True Vine

I am the vine; you are the branches. Whoever abides in me and I in him, he it is that bears much fruit, for apart from me you can do nothing. (John 15:5)

O*h, the Places You'll Go!* by Dr. Seuss is a popular gift for high school and college graduates. One of my favorite quotes from the book is:

You have brains in your head.

You have feet in your shoes.

You can steer yourself any direction you choose.

We always have a choice. It may not be easy. It may be riddled with unwanted circumstances. **But the most important choice we can make is to continue to look to and believe in the I AM.**

Which Way Is Up?

My life has often been disorienting. I have lived in six different states (three of them twice) in nineteen different residences. I have flown to multiple countries, ridden trains and buses, and driven countless miles. Hosted by many loving Christian families and sleeping in hotel rooms, I have been known to forget where I am and what day it is—or even who I am—when I awaken. Hospital waiting rooms and airports have a way of disorienting you even more. Disconnected from normal life, time becomes an elusive concept as the rest of the world carries on while you wait.

Illness, addiction, trauma... babies, graduations, new jobs... death, tragedy, loss...

In life's surreal moments, we can feel like a shell of ourselves, disengaged from everything and merely going through the motions. One person poignantly described it as "trying to catch up with yourself." Yes!

Many a young mom would echo the sentiment of "trying to catch up with yourself." For example, when someone references something from the 1980's, my mom often responds, "I don't know. That's the decade I missed while raising children."

Name an especially disorienting time you have been through in your life (a positive or negative experience). There may be more than one and this is not a competition to see whose life has been more filled with trials or celebrations.

What got you through that difficult time or transitional period?

Your Roots Are Showing

The older we get, the more trials and celebrations we go through. And what matters most is if we are rooted (Col. 2:7; Ps. 1:3).

I am going to grow old gracefully, even if it means that I have more gray hairs than my mom, which I do. As my sister put it so eloquently, "You and mom both have salt and pepper hair. Mom's is just low sodium."

Even with one of my best friends being a hairdresser, whom I know would do a great job; I refuse to be a slave to the dye. She is always begging me to let her color my hair. And no matter how many times she makes the recommendation, it is not happening.

It's not that I fear someone saying to me, "Your roots are showing," because I'd take it as a compliment.

Yes, you read that right. "Your roots are showing" can be a compliment—spiritually speaking. During the difficult times of life, does the wind get knocked out of you or are you grounded in your faith (Eph. 3:17)? Do the storms of life blow you over or are you rooted in the Word?

Take a moment today to check your roots. Spend some time in the Word and in prayer. The next time I see you, I'd love to be able to wink and say, "Your roots are showing."

What evidence do we see when our or someone else's "roots are showing"?

Getting Grounded

Seen as torture by many a teenager, "getting grounded" implies the taking away of privileges for a predetermined length of time as punishment for some wrongdoing. However, the intent is discipline, in order to guide their learning, strengthen their character, and renew their focus on the right things.

> *The negative connotation of "getting grounded" often spills into the drudgery with which we take the steps toward being grounded and rooted in the I AM.*

We can look at discipline as a list of chores or as invitations and opportunities.

What invitations and opportunities can you take advantage of this week in order to "get grounded"?

What does Revelation 22:16 say about roots?

The Divine Gardener has had a plan since the beginning of time for how we can remain in Him and invite others into relationship with Him.

Our primary text for this chapter, John 15:1-17, and the I AM declaration are an affirmation of the importance of "getting grounded," especially when we are unsure about where to go or what to do next. Before we continue, read John 15:1-17 in at least two different versions of the Bible.

What are the most repeated verbs in John 15:1-17? And how many times are they used? (Your answers may be different because of different versions of the Bible.)

Abiding and Remaining

To remain and to abide are more long-term and rooted terms than to temporarily reside. I learned that there was a difference between the questions "Where do you live?" or "Where do you stay?" for individuals whose home lives were less-than-stable. Many friends who have taken in foster children share stories of the blessing of providing a safe home for as long as is needed for the children in their care.

Yet this world is not our home, right? And since we are all children at heart, longing for a home, I would like to propose an additional refrain to *Oh, The Places You'll Go!* by Dr. Seuss.

Your house may be big.

Your house may be small.

Your house may not really be your house at all.

Make Yahweh your home.

Abide in His love.

Stay in and go out, pointing others above.

What does it look like for you to abide in the I AM who is love (1 John 4:8; John 15:9)? If you have experienced it, describe it. If you have not, express what you long for it to be in Him. Feel free to sketch what residing in the I AM's home might look like. You can make a list, quote a Bible verse, write a poem... Spend some time reflecting on and dwelling in the Presence of the I AM.

What does it look like for the I AM to abide in you? Be specific with tangible ways this can and should take place. Again, you can sketch it, make a list, quote a Bible verse, write a poem...

Reorienting Our Reactions

When the I AM abides in us, we are transformed—no matter what the circumstances.

The patient healing from heart surgery; the new mom longing for three continuous hours of sleep; the student cramming for tests; the sister holding a friend's hair back during cancer treatments; the family rocked by the tragic loss of a child; the newlywed who is navigating marriage after celebrating a wedding; the employee learning the ropes of a new job...

Impatient with ourselves in the process, it can feel easier to show anger than love, to complain rather than to find joy, to feel unsettled instead of peaceful, to be short with ourselves and others, rather than patient; easier to react than to be kind, to choose what is quick instead of what is good and right, to give up rather than remain faithful; easier to be harsh than gentle, to let it all go instead of exercising self-control.

> *Yet, if we are grounded in the I AM, looking to the LORD, believing in YHWH's name, and following His Spirit, that love, joy, peace, patience, kindness, goodness, faithfulness, gentleness, and self-control ARE possible. That is the fruit that will show in the midst of the trials.*

Go back to the paragraph in this section that starts with "Impatient..." and underline each of the aspects of the fruit of the Spirit (Gal. 5:22-23). We are known by our fruit (Matt. 7:15-23). And throughout life, we will manifest either the fruit of the Spirit or the negative fruit—through our words (James 3:9-12), our thoughts (James 1:13-15), and our actions (James 2:17-19).

Using the above verses as your inspiration, make a chart, list, or drawing on the next page, contrasting the aspects of the fruit of the Spirit with a bad habit or entrapping bad fruit.

Fruit of the Spirit[12]	Bad Fruit

Bearing Fruit

Bearing fruit, as commanded in John 15, is not merely about manifesting the fruit of the Spirit (Gal. 5:22-23).

> *When a tree or a vine bears fruit, it produces*
> *the seed from which other fruit is born.*

What is the fruit or seed that we are called to produce?

---

[12] Note: In the final chapter, we will discuss how we can live by the Spirit and the promises the I AM makes through that facet of who He is, was, and will be!

How does the teaching in John 15:1-17 parallel the words Jesus spoke before the ascension in Matthew 28:18-20?

What is necessary in order for us to bear fruit? (I found at least six specific instructions in John 15:1-17 to help us be fruit-bearing.) List below the key commands you find.

According to 1 Corinthians 3:5-9, what are our roles?

Are we responsible for the growth? How so or how not? (John 15:4-5; 1 Cor. 3:6-7)

How can we abide in the I AM *and* bear fruit? Describe how these two are correlated.

Cleaning with a Dry Sponge

Have you ever tried to clean with a dry sponge? It's impossible! It is like fingernails on the chalkboard as it scratches the surface. So, instead, we wet the sponge, and *then* use it.

But if we use and use and use the sponge without rewetting it, what happens?

Now picture a bucket of water. If we leave the sponge sitting in the water for a long time, what happens to the work that needs to be done?

Growing up in south Louisiana, you learn quickly to not leave standing water outside. It attracts mosquitos; it gets gunky and dirty; it may even start growing mold. Imagine a sponge left in that water...

Consequently, if the water remains in the sponge and the sponge remains in the water, balancing time between each, what is the result?

If we are the sponge and the bucket of water represents the Living Water, what are the applications for the I AM's teaching about abiding and fruit-bearing in John 15?

Apart from Him, We Can Do Nothing

For those who are determined to serve, reach out, work for the Lord, and do His good will, burnout is a real possibility. One cannot pour out from an empty cup. **Our testimony of belief becomes dry and brittle when we lose sight of the I AM.**

Let's renew our belief in the I AM, the Vine in whom we abide and the Love in which we dwell! Share a time when He brought about growth and fruit-bearing in your life.

A gardener or vinedresser pays special attention to all of the details—weather, soil, sun, and other conditions—in order to produce the best crop. **The Divine Gardener provides the best circumstances for each branch to remain in Him and bear fruit, even pruning when He needs to, in order to produce greater growth.**

What is the purpose of pruning and who are those that get pruned (John 15:2)?

What does "pruning" look like in our spiritual lives?

Celebrating Fruit-Bearers

One final reminder as we wrap up this lesson: **Fruit-bearing is not a competition.** We are not called to compare our growth with that of another person. The I AM Gardener and the I AM Vine have an intimate relationship with their branches, knowing what each one needs and how they can best grow fruit at any given stage of their life.

Name and describe the fruit-bearers in 2 Timothy 1:5-8.

Name two more fruit-bearers in the Bible that are an inspiration to you. (Don't forget to include the biblical reference.)

Finally, write down who your own fruit-bearers were. Who made it possible for you to be connected to the True Vine by abiding in Him and bearing the fruit of you?

There is great joy in fruit-bearing! I may not have birthed any children of my own, but I love to rejoice with my spiritual children who continue to bear fruit themselves!

Let's continue the celebration of the fruit-bearers in our lives and rejoice with our Iron Rose Sisters who continue to water our seeds of faith (Matt. 13).

> *We are each a unique branch in the Vine and a rose in God's garden.*

And we are not in it alone.

Common Threads

A characteristic of the I AM that you will **grow** rooted **and bloom** in your belief of:

Removing the **thorn** of a flawed perspective or distracted focus:

Ways in which an Iron Rose Sister can serve as **iron sharpening iron** and encourage you to **dig deeper** in your relationship with the I AM:

A verse, word of encouragement, or reminder of the I AM:

Date of completion: _____

CHAPTER 13

Who will comfort, guide, and remind me?
I AM in me, Holy Spirit living

*And I will ask the Father, and he will give you another Helper, to be with you
forever, even the Spirit of truth, whom the world cannot receive, because it
neither sees him nor knows him. You know him, for he dwells with you and
will be in you. (John 14:16-17)*

In the Old Testament, the Holy Spirit was a rare gift. The purpose
of the Holy Spirit was for anointing (kings and prophets), for
specific skills or tasks (Ex. 31:1-11), yet it was most often granted
only temporarily (Num. 11:25; 1 Sam. 16:14). Very few individuals were
blessed with the indwelling presence of the Holy Spirit for life (e.g.
John the Baptist, Luke 1:15).

Even David feared that the Spirit of the LORD would be stripped
from him as it was from Saul (1 Sam. 16:13-14; Ps. 51). Moses, whose
life we have examined at length through this book, was honored to be
in the presence of the LORD, but we do not see clear evidence that the
Spirit dwelled in him.

177

Therefore, belief in the Holy Spirit, for the disciples of Jesus, was a challenge. They were not familiar with His work. They looked to the Old Testament, just as we can look to the book of Acts, for examples. Yet, as happened with the disciples, we often misunderstand or fear the work of the Holy Spirit.

Before we go to the New Testament and glean additional understanding of the Holy Spirit, allow me to share the following poem, written after being inspired by the work of the Holy Spirit in the Old Testament.

In Hebrew, the word for the Spirit of the LORD is *Ruach*. It is pronounced as the sound of a rushing wind and therefore is an onomatopoeia, like "swoosh" or "plop," a word that sounds like what it means.

We cannot see the wind, but we see the effect of what it does and how it moves. We cannot see the Spirit, but we witness what He does, how He moves, and we believe in Him. Do you believe in the Holy Spirit?

RUACH

By Michelle J. Goff

He hovered over the waters... *Ruach*.
And the Spirit of the LORD kept moving, never dormant... **Ruach!**
Descended as a cloud and a pillar of fire to guide; a cloud again, resting on the elders to prophesy... *Ruach*.
Imparted wisdom to Joshua, judges, and kings; Gideon blew a trumpet, Samson defeated foes... the Spirit of the LORD came powerfully upon them... **Ruach!**
Poured out to prophesy, lead, judge, and rule... wisdom and understanding characterized the Spirit's presence in the lives of the anointed... *Ruach*.

Anointed as God's chosen kings, Saul, David, and Solomon were inspired by the Spirit to speak, were filled by the Spirit to lead, and were empowered by the Spirit to defeat the enemy... **Ruach!**
But the Spirit of the LORD departed from Saul. *Silence.*
Disobedience, rejection, an enemy of the LORD ... *Silence.*
David bore witness to the tormented evil spirit in Saul; the absence of the Spirit of the LORD. *Silence.*
"Take not your Holy Spirit from me," **Ruach!**
David experienced the indwelling of the Spirit... *Ruach.*
May the Spirit of the LORD rest upon me... *Ruach.*
May He pour out wisdom, understanding, counsel, and might, knowledge and fear of the LORD ... **Ruach!**
Who can fathom the Spirit of the LORD? May I never tire of the quest to contemplate Him and His presence... *Ruach.*
Use me to proclaim good news to the poor; bind up the brokenhearted; proclaim freedom for the captives and release from darkness for the prisoners.
Ruach, breathe new life into me as you did for the faithful of old.
Guide me in your ways and instruct my plans.
Come upon me powerfully and speak through me as you did through the prophets of another day. **Ruach!**
I do not expect a double portion like Elisha, but that I may rest in Your presence, taste of your goodness, and never experience the pain of your departure.
Ruach... Ruach... **Ruach!**

Share any comments, reflections, or your own testimony of belief about the Holy Spirit in the Old Testament.

The Holy Spirit in the New Testament

What do we learn about the Holy Spirit from the following New Testament passages?

Hebrews 2:4

John 16:7-15

Acts 1:1-5

Acts 2:1-4

Acts 2:38

Our limited minds cannot comprehend the I AM's limitless nature. Yet one of the Spirit's specific roles is to bring us into a deeper understanding of who the I AM *already* is.

> [25] *"These things I have spoken to you while I am still with you.* [26] *But the Helper, the Holy Spirit, whom the Father will send in my name, he will teach you all things and bring to your remembrance all that I have said to you.* (John 14:25-26)

What is the most vital and encouraging facet of the Holy Spirit in your life today? There is no right or wrong answer because the I AM is big enough to be all things to all people at all times. This is an opportunity to explain how He is working in your life right now—whether you see Him or understand all of what He is doing and being or not.

Greater Things

"Truly, truly, I say to you, whoever believes in me will also do the works that I do; and greater works than these will he do, because I am going to the Father." (John 14:12)

How are we to accomplish these "greater things"? (See John 14:12-17.)

Do you believe in the I AM, Holy Spirit? What do you believe about Him?

Remembering to Believe When We Forget

Belief is the pivotal key on which the rest of life hinges. Yet our belief wavers; we doubt. We forget what and in Whom we believe.

Thankfully, the I AM assures us that we will not be alone in our belief and in our doubts. We have the Helper, the Counselor, the Advocate, the Holy Spirit to comfort, guide, and remind us (John 14, 16).

What happens in John 20:24-29? And how does Jesus react?

John places this story of Jesus as the final point before affirming the purpose of his gospel account.

> *"...these are written so that you may believe that Jesus is the Christ, the Son of God, and that by believing you may have life in his name"* (John 20:31).

What have you learned about YHWH's name and the power of believing in the I AM?

By way of review, how does the Holy Spirit point us to the I AM and the answers to the questions that we have addressed throughout the chapters of this book? **Choose three of the questions listed below** and allow the Spirit to lead you to the comfort, truth, guidance, affirmation, conviction, or assistance you need.

Be sure to include an "I AM statement" in each of your responses and feel free to weave the various ways in which the Spirit brings about His reminders into your answers. They may be through songs, specific Bible verses, drawings, poems, stories... These are additional elements of your testimony of belief!

I am intentionally leaving more than a page of blank space for you to complete this exercise. Take your time with it. Dedicate this time in the Presence of the I AM to Him. Thank Him for giving His Spirit to help you through this process and through every day of your life.

And if you have not yet been united with the I AM through baptism and therefore do not yet have the Holy Spirit dwelling in you, I would like to personally invite you to publicly declare your belief that Jesus is the Son of God, the I AM who became flesh and dwelt among us, to repent of your past way of life, to confess Him as Lord of your life, and be baptized into His name for the forgiveness of sins and that you might receive the gift of the Holy Spirit.

Remember, choose three of the questions below to respond to, allowing the Holy Spirit to guide you into reminders of the I AM and a deeper testimony of belief in Him. Feel free to refer back to your notes from the chapters of this book. The chapter numbers correspond with the question numbers below.

1. How can you keep your eyes fixed on the I AM?

2. What is the impact the One who was and is and is to come makes in your life?

3. How can you remember that it's not about "who am I?", but rather who the I AM is?

4. What do you need to believe that the I AM *already* is _____, in order to remember that you are _____?

5. How can you ask for a drink?

6. Will your needs be met?

7. Are you seeing clearly?

8. Are you safe?

9. Does anyone truly know you?

10. Where do you find hope?

11. Who do you believe?

12. Where do you go from here?

(intentionally blank for continued responses to the three selected questions)

Testimonies of Belief in the I AM

One of the things that most affirms God's faithfulness and the other facets of His character, as revealed through His name, are God stories. "God stories," as I call them, are real life accounts of ways in which we have seen the LORD work and give Him the glory for what He has done. These God stories become our testimonies of belief—manifestations of the incarnation of the I AM. The more the Spirit helps us recognize the I AM's work, the greater our belief and more solid our testimony becomes, as you experienced through the previous exercise.

The Holy Spirit reminds me of God stories when I feel weak or discouraged. Consequently, my testimony of belief is strengthened and encouraged through the God stories in Scripture, in my own life, and in the lives of others. Thank you for sharing your testimony of belief with your Iron Rose Sisters and allowing yourself to be encouraged and challenged by their stories as well!

Common Threads

This is our final opportunity to share in the Common Threads in the context of this book. Be sure to spend extra time in prayer together over the Common Threads when you gather in your small group.

A name or characteristic of the I AM that you will **grow and bloom** in your belief of:

Removing the **thorn** of a flawed perspective or distracted focus:

Ways in which an Iron Rose Sister can serve as **iron sharpening iron** and encourage you to **dig deeper** in your relationship with the I AM:

A verse, word of encouragement, or reminder of the I AM:

Date of completion: _____

Conclusion

Throughout this book, we have explored the meaning of YHWH's name, I AM or LORD, and the various ways in which He has revealed Himself throughout Scripture and in our own lives. It is my prayer that through these testimonies of belief, your belief in the I AM has grown and your own testimony has blossomed.

When Moses asked who he should tell Pharaoh and the Israelites had sent him, God responded with His name, "I AM who I AM" or "I WILL BE who I WILL BE" (Ex. 3:14-15). Normally, the verb "is" requires an object (whether spoken or implied), unless it is in answer to a question. For example, if I were to say "I am..." you would wait, expecting me to finish the sentence. Maybe "I am tired," or "I am a Christian," or "I am Michelle."

God does not follow those rules because without Him nothing else would even exist. He is. He was. He will be. He exists. All existence stems from Him.

> **Who He is, is that He is.**

YHWH, Yahweh, LORD goes beyond any title or characteristic we assign Him or through which He uncovers who and how He is. The other "names" we see for YHWH throughout the Bible demonstrate the ways in which the LORD reveals Himself and YHWH invites us into relationship, through the I AM incarnate—all manifestations of His existence as the Great I AM.

Yet, did you know that the expression "The Great I AM" does not appear in the Bible? This phrase that we have adopted, even in the title of this book, comes from a famous hymn, "Our God, He is Alive," written by Aaron Wesley Dicus. A preacher, physicist, and college professor, he composed many songs that are still sung to this day. Through the words of this hymn, praise is offered to God for His greatness both in the physical and spiritual realms, affirming that nothing would exist without Him. Everything else He did, does, and will do proclaims His desire for relationship with us through belief in Him.

The phrase "the Great I AM" is an attempt to elevate the affirmation of His existence. Through the hymn, "Our God, He Is Alive," especially since it was written by a man of science, we hear a resounding affirmation of the existence of God. It is Mr. Dicus' testimony of belief.

Our God, He Is Alive[13]

There is, beyond the azure blue
A God, concealed from human sight.
He tinted skies with heav'nly hue
And framed the worlds with His great might.

Chorus:
There is a God (There is a God), He is alive (He is alive).
In Him we live (In Him we live) and we survive (and we survive).
From dust our God (From dust our God) created man (created man).
He is our God (He is our God), the Great I AM (the Great I AM).

There was a long, long time ago
A God whose voice the prophets heard
He is the God that we should know
Who speaks from His inspired word.

Our God, whose Son upon a tree
A life was willing there to give
That He from sin might set man free
And evermore with Him could live.

---

13 The words and music to "Our God, He Is Alive" were copyrighted in 1966 by A. W. Dicus and assigned in 1973 to Sacred Selections Inc., Ellis J. Crum, owner, Kendallville, IN 46755.

We Believe!

As A.W. Dicus did through his hymn, our testimonies of belief are proclamations of the existence of the I AM in the world and in our personal lives. Your testimony of belief may not make it into a hymnbook or be sung by hundreds of thousands of people. Yet your testimony of belief can serve as an invitation for others to believe, as an affirmation of belief for those whose belief is wavering, and as a proclamation of belief in a time of personal doubt.

When we fix our eyes on the I AM and look with eyes of faith, we remember to see things from His perspective. Remember: Nothing exists without YHWH. And for those who are in Him, we can rest, assured in our belief, not because of who we are, but because of Who He *already* is.

We already are because the I AM already is, was, and always will be.

As you conclude your time together with your Iron Rose Sisters through this interactive Bible study book, spend some time in prayer together, rejoicing over the I AM and solidifying our belief in His name.

The good news (gospel) of our testimonies is that the I AM dwells in us— the ultimate incarnation of the I AM for others!

Final Charge: Sharing Your Testimony of Belief

Throughout this book, you have practiced sharing your testimony of belief with your Iron Rose Sisters. As a ministry, we would love to hear your story, as well! Whether you write it out as a narrative of your relationship with the I AM, compose a song and sing it, record a video of yourself sharing your testimony of belief, or have created a piece of artwork that reflects your journey of belief in the I AM, we want to help you share that story!

Please send a copy to our email: ironrosesister@gmail.com, tag us on Facebook "Iron Rose Sister Ministries" or on Instagram @ironrosesister

Blessings in your belief and thanks for joining me on the journey.

Looking forward to hearing from you!

M.

About the Author

Michelle J. Goff has been writing small group Bible study materials in English and in Spanish throughout her ministry career. God has led Michelle to share these resources with more women across the world through Iron Rose Sister Ministries, a registered non-profit. She also continues to take advantage of opportunities for speaking engagements, seminars, women's retreats, and other women's ministry events across the Americas, in both English and in Spanish. If you would like to book a seminar in your area, please contact Michelle at ironrosesister@gmail.com, or for more information, visit www.IronRoseSister.com.

Personal Life

Michelle grew up in Baton Rouge, Louisiana, with her parents and three younger sisters. Her love and desire for helping women in their journey began early with her sisters, even when they thought she was being bossy. They've all grown a lot from those early years, but the sisterly bonds remain. Michelle has been blessed by the support of her family through all of her endeavors over the years.

Michelle enjoys time with family, cheering on the Atlanta Braves and the Louisiana State University Tigers, having coffee or tea with friends, movies, travel, and speaking Spanish. And guess what her favorite flower is? Yep. The red rose.

She currently resides in Searcy, Arkansas, near her parents.

Ministry and Educational Experience

Michelle first felt called into ministry during her senior year at Harding University while obtaining a Bachelor of Arts degree in Communication Disorders and Spanish. She planned to join a team to plant a church in north Bogotá, Colombia, so she moved to Atlanta after graduating in May 1999 to facilitate that church-plant. Even though the plan for a Bogotá team fell through, Michelle continued her dream to be a part of a church plant there, which happened in March 2000.

She worked in the missions ministry at the North Atlanta Church of Christ for eighteen months before moving to Denver to work with English- and Spanish-speaking church plants there (Highlands Ranch Church of Christ and three Spanish-speaking congregations). During her two-and-a-half years there, Michelle continued her involvement in Bogotá and throughout various regions of Venezuela, visiting new church plants, teaching classes, conducting women's retreats, and speaking at and volunteering with youth camps.

In March 2003, Michelle moved to Caracas, Venezuela, to assist with a church planting on the eastern side of the city. Her time in Caracas was focused on the East Caracas congregation, but she was also able to participate in other women's activities across the country. In the four years Michelle spent in Caracas, the congregation grew from the twelve people meeting in her apartment to almost 100 meeting in a hotel conference room. The East Caracas congregation continues to meet in spite of the difficult economic and political situation in the country. A visit to Bogotá every three months to renew her Venezuelan visa also facilitated continued assistance with the North Bogotá congregation. And Michelle has rejoiced in that congregation's growth and the fact that they have helped start at least one additional congregation since then.

In March 2007, Michelle transitioned back into ministry in the United States as the women's campus minister for the South Baton Rouge Church of Christ at the Christian Student Center (CSC) near the LSU campus. While walking with the college students on their spiritual journey and serving in other women's ministry roles, Michelle also pursued her "nerdy passion" of Spanish. She graduated from LSU in December 2011 with a Masters in Hispanic Studies,

Linguistics Concentration. Her thesis explored the influence of social and religious factors in the interpretation of Scripture.

Michelle is now following God's calling to use her bilingual ministry experience with women of all ages and cultural backgrounds to bless them with opportunities for growth and deep spiritual connection with other Christian sisters through Iron Rose Sister Ministries.

Equipping, encouraging, and empowering women—an excellent summary of Iron Rose Sister Ministries' vision and Michelle's passion. Thanks for your prayers for her and for the fulfillment of that mission.

About Iron Rose Sister
Ministries

Vision:

To equip women to connect to God and one another more deeply in English, Spanish, and bilingual contexts, across the Americas.

Overall Mission:

A ministry that facilitates Christian sister relationships that will be like iron sharpening iron, encouraging and inspiring each other to be as beautiful as a rose in spite of a few thorns. One of its goals is to provide women's Bible studies that are simple enough for anyone to lead and yet, deep enough for everyone to grow. These resources are available in English and Spanish (Iron Rose Sister Ministries - IRSM/Ministerio Hermana Rosa de Hierro - MHRH).

FACETS of Iron Rose Sister Ministries' Vision:

F – Faithfulness – to God above all else. First and foremost: *"Seek first His kingdom and His righteousness and all these things will be added to you as well"* (Matt. 6:33).

197

A – Authenticity – We're not hypocrites, just human. *"But he said to me, "My grace is sufficient for you, for my power is made perfect in weakness." Therefore I will boast all the more gladly about my weaknesses, so that Christ's power may rest on me. That is why, for Christ's sake, I delight in weaknesses, in insults, in hardships, in persecutions, in difficulties. For when I am weak, then I am strong"* (2 Cor. 12:9-10).

C – Community – We were not created to have an isolated relationship with God. He has designed the church as a body with many parts (1 Cor. 12). The magnitude of "one another" passages in the New Testament affirms this design. As women, we have unique relational needs at various stages in life—whether we are going through a time in which we need, like Moses, our arms raised in support by others (Ex. 17:12) or are able to rejoice with those who rejoice and mourn with those who mourn (Rom. 12:15). The Iron Rose Sister Ministries studies are designed to be shared in community.

E – Encouragement through Prayer and Accountability – *"As iron sharpens iron, so one person sharpens another"* (Prov. 27:17). God has not left us alone in this journey. *"Confess your sins to each other and pray for each other so that you may be healed. The prayer of a righteous man is powerful and effective"* (James 5:16). It is our prayer that every woman that joins in this mission participates as an Iron Rose Sister with other women, partnering in prayer and loving accountability.

T – Testimony – We all have a "God story." By recognizing his living and active hand in our lives, we are blessed to share that message of hope with others (John 4:39-42). Thankfully, that story is not over! God continues to work in the transformation of lives, and we long to hear your story.

S – Study – *"The Word of God is alive and active. Sharper than any double-edged sword, it penetrates even to dividing soul and spirit, joints and marrow; it judges the thoughts and attitudes of the heart"* (Heb. 4:12).

In order to fully realize the blessing, benefit, and design of the Iron Rose Sister Ministries vision, we must go to the

Creator. Through a greater knowledge of the Word, we can blossom as roses and remove a few thorns—discerning the leading of the Spirit, recognizing the voice of the Father, and following the example of the Son. This is more effectively accomplished in community (small group Bible studies), but not to the exclusion of time alone with God (personal Bible study).

For more information, please:

Visit www.IronRoseSister.com

Sign up for the IRSM blog and monthly newsletter.

IRSM is a registered 501(c)(3) public nonprofit with a board of directors and advisory eldership.

Bibliography

Evans, Rachel Held. *Inspired*. Nashville: Nelson Books, 2018.

Swindoll, Charles R. *The Swindoll Study Bible*. Carol Stream, Illinois: Tyndale House Publishers, 2017.

Swindoll, Charles R. "Insights on John," *Swindoll Living Insights New Testament Commentary*, Volume 4. Carol Stream, Illinois: Tyndale House Publishers, 2014.

The Lion King. Walt Disney Pictures, 1994.

Tozer A. W. *The Pursuit of God*. Chicago: Moody Publishers, 2015.

West, John. "How Hollywood reinvented C.S. Lewis in the film "Shadowlands."" Last modified July 2, 2012. http://www.cslewisweb.com/2012/07/how-hollywood-reinvented-c-s-lewis-in-the-film-shadowlands/

Facilitator's Guide

As presented in the *Iron Rose Sister Ministries Bible Studies Format*, the group is encouraged to rotate who leads the discussion each week.

Even if you do not feel equipped to facilitate the discussion or feel that you lack adequate experience to do so, it is a rich opportunity for growth and blessing. You are among sisters and friends that are supporting you in this part of your journey, as well.

Tips or reminders, especially for new leaders:

➤ Make it your own and allow the Spirit to lead—these studies are a resource, not a script.
  - Select which questions you would like to discuss, and plan for ones you might need to skip if you are running short on time.
  - You are welcome to add questions of your own or highlight portions of the chapter that most impacted you, whether they were designated for discussion or not.
  - Note: More times than not, for time reasons, you will not be able to cover every question in the entire chapter together each week.

➤ Include additional examples from Scripture and encourage others to do the same.
  - Online Bible programs such as BibleGateway.com or BlueLetterBible.org provide excellent resources like multiple versions of the Bible, concordances (to look up the occurrences of a word), Bible dictionaries, and commentaries.

➤ Be willing to answer the designated discussion questions first, using your own examples, but avoid the temptation to do all the talking.

- o Allow for awkward silence to provide the opportunity for others to share. Tip: Counting to 10 in your head gives others a chance to think about their answers. Feel free to reword the question, as well.
- o It's okay to call on someone and encourage them to answer a specific question.
- o "Why or why not?" or "Can you add to that comment?" are good follow-up questions for discussion.

➢ Leading is about facilitating the discussion, not about having all the answers.

- o When someone brings up a difficult situation or a challenging question, you can always open it up to the group for answers from Scripture, not just personal advice.
- o The answer may merit further Bible study or the consultation of someone with more experience in the Word and/or experience regarding that type of situation. That's okay! We're digging deeper.

➢ Affirm and encourage group participation.

- o One of the best ways to facilitate continued conversation and discussion is to affirm the others in the group. Even if you don't agree with what is stated, you can appreciate their willingness to share their thoughts.
- o Thank those who were willing to read passages of Scripture, to pray, and to ask questions in order to dig deeper. And don't forget to thank those who participated by sharing their answers and input during the discussion.
- o If someone is talking too much or over-sharing, you can gently interrupt and thank her for sharing. It may be appropriate to lead a prayer over her or the situation in that moment in order to move forward with the week's topic.

➤ Accommodate for larger groups, as needed.
  o The ideal small group size is 6-8 women. If your group is larger, more reserved women will be less likely to share.
  o For groups larger than 6-8 women, in order to facilitate a deeper connection with one another and with the I AM through that week's discussion, here are a few suggestions:
    ▪ Choose a section of the chapter or specific questions that can be answered in mini-groups (2-3 people).
    ▪ Allow for time in those mini-group discussions and then bring the entire group back together. This can be done multiple times during the week's study.
    ▪ Also, the mini-groups can be a good way to share in the Common Threads and/or in prayer.
➤ Give a practical wrap-up conclusion or "take-home" application from the week as you close with the Common Threads.
➤ Be sure to budget some time for prayer.
➤ Remember our purposes as students of the Word and daughters of the King. We are striving to listen and to deepen our relationships with the I AM and one another—to be Iron Rose Sisters that serve as iron sharpening iron as we encourage one another to be as beautiful as a rose in spite of a few thorns.

Notes/Testimonies

Notes/Testimonies

www.ingramcontent.com/pod-product-compliance
Lightning Source LLC
LaVergne TN
LVHW011347080426
835511LV00005B/164